Growth, Gardens, & Grace

Spring Devotionals Inspired by God's Creation

Growth, Gardens, & Grace

Spring Devotionals Inspired by God's Creation

Growth, Gardens, & Grace: Spring Devotionals Inspired by God's Creation

Rooted & Flourishing Devotional Series

Copyright © 2023 by Andrea L. Robinson

All rights reserved. No part of this publication may be reproduced, stored in a retrieval system, or transmitted in any form or by any means—electronic, mechanical, photocopy, recording, or any other—except for brief quotations in printed reviews, without the prior permission of the publisher.

Scripture quotations are taken from the Holy Bible, New Living Translation, copyright ©1996, 2004, 2015 by Tyndale House Foundation. Used by permission of Tyndale House Publishers, Carol Stream, Illinois 60188. All rights reserved.

MCGAHAN PUBLISHING HOUSE | LYNCHBURG, TENNESSEE

www.mphbooks.com

Requests for information should be sent to:

info@mphbooks.com

Cover Design by Marynn Spurlock & Andrew Waters

Photos & Graphics by Kaleigh Madison LLC

ISBN 978-1-951252-25-0

For my Pops, who taught me that nature is the best medicine

Contents

Acknowledgements   9

Introduction & Instructions   11

Daily Devotionals   13

Acknowledgements

I'm overwhelmed by the love and support of the people God has placed in my life. Words can't express the extent to which I am thankful for my family and friends. To Wesley, you are my North Star, soulmate, and best friend. From emotional support to devotional feedback to household upkeep, I couldn't function without you. To Asher, my favorite surprise and faithful assistant, thank you for remaining patient and peaceful despite my frenetic pace. Your attention to detail and organizational skills equip me to accomplish exponentially more than I could alone. To Abel, the life of the party and heart of our family, your love keeps my priorities in order and gives me the confidence to reach goals beyond my imagination. To all of my family and friends, thank you for allowing me to share your best moments, worst moments, and everything in between. Your encouragement strengthens me more than you know, and my life is enriched because you are part of it. To my dear friends Tom and Lisa Buckle and Doug and Melissa Sittason, thank you for remaining faithful friends despite my periodic disappearances due to devotional writing. To Lynn Ferrell, you are a constant source of wisdom in my life, and your feedback on these devotionals will bless each person who reads them. To Hollie Sipe, I treasure your words of encouragement as much as your editing skills, which are substantial. Both have made this volume substantially better. To the many friends who've supported the launch of Rooted and Flourishing—Amanda, Amy, Brian, Bridget, Brittani, Jessy, Karen,

Acknowledgements

Kim, Laura, Tonya, Mike, and Veneranda—I'm honored by your faith in these devotionals and your willingness to share them with others. To my graphic designer/photographer/media expert, Kaleigh McGinn, I'm thankful for your endless patience and awed at your ability to make my wild ideas look professional. To my pastors, Spencer and Ellen Beach, thank you for continuing to champion my work and pour wisdom into my life. Your leadership has equipped me to grow in every aspect of my life and ministry. For Caleb Poston and McGahan Publishing, I want to express sincere gratitude once again. Your dialogue and feedback have brought my vision for these devotionals to life and made them better along the way. Finally, thank you to Jesus, my Lord and Friend. I pray that my own imperfect efforts honor you and edify your people.

Introduction & Instructions

Hello friends,

If you read the autumn or winter volume of Rooted & Flourishing, I hope you feel like you're returning to spend time with a friend. With each devotional I write, I imagine sharing my stories with you face-to-face, and I pray for God to work in your heart. As these spring devotionals revolve around *Growth, Gardens, & Grace*, I invite you to walk through my garden and learn from the lessons God has taught me there.

In case this is the first book you're reading in the Rooted & Flourishing series, let me briefly introduce myself. I am a wife, mom, pastor, scholar, adventurer, fitness fanatic, and avid gardener. I'm far from perfect, but I love Jesus, I love to learn, and I seize every day with joy. Despite my qualifications as a scholar, I'm quite irresponsible and impulsive. Nonetheless, God allows me to serve Him in ways that astound me.

In January 2020 as I was fasting, I felt God compelling me to write a series of devotions inspired by nature. Although I was excited about the prospect of writing devotionals, I simply wasn't sure when I would have time to write them. As a pastor, wife, and mom of two boys, my schedule didn't exactly provide large blocks of writing time. Unbeknownst to me, God was already orchestrating the circumstances under which I would be writing devotionals on a daily basis.

As we now know, 2020 was the year in which we encountered the coronavirus, a quarantine, and an unprecedented degree of isolation. In an effort to encourage our church family, our church staff decided to produce daily devotionals, and I lead the project. Initially,

Introductions & Instructions

I didn't make the connection between the devotionals God was calling me to write and the devotionals I was writing for our church. As time passed, however, I realized that God was helping me sow the seeds of my devotional project.

You now hold in your hands the spring installment of the Rooted & Flourishing series. Although many of the devotionals in this volume are inspired by the natural world, we'll also discuss deep Scriptural themes, such as the death and resurrection of Jesus and his future return. As you read devotions about our Savior and the world he created, I pray that you become more deeply rooted in God's presence and flourish in your life's journey.

Before you begin, allow me to offer a few suggestions. Each day, I've provided a devotional, a brief prayer, and a prompt for reflection, meditation, or application. I pray that each will serve as a launching point for further prayer, introspection, and growth. In some instances, I've recommended a passage of Scripture for further reading, and in those cases a QR code has been provided for convenient access to the chapters or verses. For all Scripture passages cited in the devotionals, I've used the New Living Translation with the exception of verses I translated myself.

I've also included blank space for journaling. I will occasionally suggest journaling cues, but the space is primarily for you to write your thoughts on how the devotional impacted you or truths God is impressing upon your soul. As you pray, meditate, and journal, take time to listen for the still, small voice of God. Give him permission to uproot any weeds in the garden of your life, create fertile soil for new growth, and plant the seeds of his will.

– Andrea

Be sure to connect with me at **www.AndreaLeighRobinson.org** and on social media. I have additional content and interactive opportunities waiting for you!

Day 1
Spring into a New Season

Life flows in seasons, and spring has finally arrived! I'm sure you aren't surprised that my favorite season is spring. I'm delighted when the weather begins to warm and the first tiny shoots peek above the ground. I'm jubilant when my garden begins to transform from dull browns to lush greens.

Solomon, likewise, celebrated the dawning of spring. He rejoiced over the changing season and invited his beloved to share his joy.

Look, the winter is past,
and the rains are over and gone.
The flowers are springing up,
the season of singing birds has come,
and the cooing of turtledoves fills the air.
The fig trees are forming young fruit,
and the fragrant grapevines are blossoming.
Rise up, my darling!
Come away with me, my fair one!
Song of Songs 2:11–13

Whether Solomon used his poetic skills to describe the literal changing of seasons or the flowering of young love, his words convey the same basic concept. Just as the natural world is revitalized and refreshed each spring, God prepares us to flourish anew in each season. He can restore barren parts of our souls and cause stagnant places to

Day 1

bear fruit. He can even bring new growth and greater yield to soil that is already rich and productive.

As the seasons of the natural world change, I challenge you to move into a new season of spiritual and personal growth. As for the nature of your growth, only God knows and only you can discern. I pray the devotionals in this volume will facilitate your spiritual formation and help you grow ever closer to the heart of your Father. Listen for his voice, walk in his will, and rejoice as you bear new fruit. Perhaps, like Solomon, you'll even invite a friend or loved one to join you on your journey.

Lord, thank you for offering new opportunities for growth throughout the changing seasons of my life. I'm grateful for your steadfast love and guidance, which remain constant in every season. I ask you to refresh my mind and so that I can serve you with joy and walk in the fullness of your love. Give me a greater capacity to discern your voice and obey your will so that nothing hinders my growth. Reveal areas of my life in which you are calling me to mature or yield a greater measure of fruit. Surround me by your presence and people who will draw me closer to you. In Jesus' name, Amen.

Personal Reflection

Pray for God's guidance as you seek growth in this season. Consider whether he might be leading you to develop skills, gain knowledge, grow relationally, or mature spiritually. Write your thoughts below.

_____

_____

_____

Growth, Gardens, & Grace

Day 2
Happy Little Bluebirds

A family of bluebirds nests in the birdhouse on my back fence each spring. One of my favorite spring activities is watching them prepare their temporary home and raise hatchlings. My heart is filled with peace and joy as I sit on my back patio watching the little birds flit to and fro.

One spring, as my birds were preparing their nest, I noticed that their progress was *very* leisurely. They would fly away and come back with one small piece of straw, place it in the birdhouse, then sit on the fence for a while. They would eventually fly from the fence to the tree, hop around, then depart to retrieve more material for the nest. I marveled at how unhurried they were, how happy they seemed to be, and how nonchalant they were about completing their task. Their behavior immediately made me think of the familiar verse, in which Jesus says to his followers:

> That is why I tell you not to worry about everyday life—whether you have enough food and drink, or enough clothes to wear. Isn't life more than food, and your body more than clothing? Look at the birds. They don't plant or harvest or store food in barns, for your heavenly Father feeds them. And aren't you far more valuable to him than they are? Can all your worries add a single moment to your life?
>
> *Matthew 6:25–27*

My bluebirds provided a clear illustration of Jesus' words. They weren't anxious about finishing their nest. They weren't stockpiling food for later. As far as I could tell, they weren't worried about a thing. We could learn a lot about *not* worrying from the birds!

Jesus instructs us not to worry because worry undermines our relationship with the Father. When we worry, we doubt God's love and his ability to provide. Yet, Jesus reminds us that we are valuable to our Father—more valuable than the birds, for whom he faithfully provides! And let me assure you, the birds are thriving. They always complete their nest on time, they never run out of food, and their blue feathers provide stunningly beautiful vestment.

God owns the world and everything in it (Psalm 50:12). He certainly has enough resources to provide for your every need. So, every time you see the birds living their care-free lives, remember that God's provision is unfailing.

Father, thank you for your constant provision and protection. Help me release my worries and anxieties to you today. Give me faith that cannot be shaken and grow my trust in your promises. I confess and believe that you own the world and everything in it. Help me stand firm on your steadfast love and entrust every need to you. Give me wisdom as I steward the resources you entrust to my care. In Jesus' name, Amen.

Personal Reflection

Take some time to ask God whether you have allowed any worries to take root in your heart. Ask Him to reveal any specific areas in which you might be failing to trust in his provision. Ask Him if any perceived lack of provision could be corrected by managing your resources more wisely.

Day 2

Day 3
Worry Woes — Part 1

Yesterday we discussed Jesus' exhortation not to worry. I told you about the care-free bluebirds that live in my yard, which remind me that God's provision and protection are unfailing. When we worry, we expose a lack of faith in our heart that keeps us from a deep and abiding relationship with our Father. When we trust him, however, we get to experience his loving care, and our faith has an opportunity to grow.

Our wise Father cautions against worry not only because it is spiritually detrimental, but also because it's harmful to our health. Anxiety can cause a plethora of physiological issues, beginning with insomnia, which creates its own downward spiral of physical and mental problems. Worry can cause stomach pain, nausea, and digestive problems. It causes the nervous system to release stress hormones, which can result in fatigue, dizziness, headaches, shortness of breath, muscle tension, and high blood pressure. Worry weakens the body's immune system and makes us susceptible to other illnesses. Pathological worry can even cause permanent damage to the brain, leading to cognitive impairment and neurodegenerative diseases.

I can personally attest to some of these symptoms from my time in graduate school. During one particularly challenging semester leading to the completion of my coursework and dissertation proposal, I began having unexplainable physical maladies. My throat felt so swollen I had trouble swallowing. I felt like a lead weight was resting on my chest. My heart even began to beat irregularly at times.

As a normally serene person, I was certain my physical symptoms were the result of a serious illness. Was I having a heart attack? Did I have throat cancer? After a trip to the ER and numerous doctor visits, however, no physiological problems could be identified. Despite my adamant insistence that I was not stressed-out, the doctors diagnosed me with anxiety. Looking back, I can see that they were absolutely correct.

Although the ancient authors of Scripture lacked the insights of modern medicine, even they knew worry is bad for our physical health. According to Proverbs 14:30, "A peaceful heart leads to a healthy body," and in Ecclesiastes 11:10, we are advised, "refuse to worry, and keep your body healthy."

As beings who are composed of physical and spiritual elements, every aspect of our self impacts the other aspects. Thus, mental-emotional struggles like worry have a detrimental impact on our physical and spiritual health.

Our Father offers us a life of hope and health. We simply have to trust him enough to receive it. We'll discuss strategies for overcoming worry tomorrow, but let's pause, pray, and reflect before we go further.

Father, thank you for protecting me and providing for my needs. Forgive me for failing to trust in your care. I repent of wasting my time and energy on worry. Teach me to guard my mental, spiritual, and physical health diligently. Help me to better steward my mental and physical capacities by refusing to worry. Grow my faith and teach me strategies for managing my mental, emotional, and physical health. Guide me into a deeper relationship with you as I learn to rest in your care. When my mind is

Day 3

tempted to dwell on anxious thoughts, I ask that you would gently redirect my focus toward your lovingkindness. In Jesus' name, Amen.

Personal Reflection

Prayerfully reflect upon your capacity for managing stress. Do you worry to the extent that you experience physical symptoms? Do you struggle to enjoy today because you are worried about tomorrow? We'll discuss specific strategies for managing worry tomorrow, but for now simply share your struggles with God and ask him to grow your faith.

_____

_____

_____

_____

_____

_____

_____

_____

_____

_____

_____

_____

Day 4
Worry Woes — Part 2

The last couple of days, we've discussed our difficult-to-overcome propensity to worry. As we discussed, the author of Ecclesiastes instructs that we should "refuse to worry," (Ecclesiastes 11:10), but how do we accomplish that? Peter teaches, "Give all your worries and cares to God, for he cares about you," (1 Peter 5:7). But, still, what does it look like to give our cares to God? Although *not* worrying is certainly easier said than done, we can take constructive steps to manage anxious thoughts.

Willpower alone simply isn't enough to overcome our anxious thoughts. Like any aspect of spiritual growth, releasing our worries to God is a matter of prayer and practice. In fact, worry can sometimes be a signal that we need to take decisive action. So, our initial step should be to determine whether we can enact any proactive measures to resolve the source of our concern. Do we need to finish a project over which we've been procrastinating? Do we need to come clean about a lie we've told? Do we need to address a bad habit that is causing physical concerns? As we prayerfully assess the situation, the Lord might show us an avenue of productive resolution.

Once we do everything in our power to address the source of the stress, we must also build the spiritual stamina to overcome our worries. We, thus, learn to abide in the presence of God through prayer. We continually confess our concerns to him and allow him to reaffirm his promises. At the same time, we must foster a regular practice of

Day 4

Scripture reading and memorization so that God can bring his promises to our minds as we need them. Finally, we must take each thought (i.e., worry) captive and submit it to God (2 Corinthians 10:5). Each time an anxious thought rises to the surface, we should replace it with the truth of Scripture.

Learning to cast our cares upon the Lord takes practice and persistence. You may not notice progress for days, months, or even years, but if you are diligent, you'll one day look back and realize how far you've come! Remember, I know from experience!

Father, thank you for creating a good and perfect plan for my life. Help me to trust in your goodness as you lead me into the purpose for which you've created me. Teach me to better steward my mental, emotional, physical, and spiritual health. Equip me to be proactive about finding solutions to my concerns while also relinquishing my worries to you. Guide me into a deeper relationship with you as I learn to rest in your care. When my mind is tempted to dwell on anxious thoughts, I ask that you would gently redirect my focus toward your lovingkindness. In Jesus' name, Amen.

Personal Reflection

Consider the four strategies we discussed above: (1) taking proactive measures, (2) confessing our cares to God, (3) reading and memorizing Scripture, and (4) replacing anxious thoughts with the truth of God. Determine which ones are most difficult for you and begin working on one or more of them today. If you need help getting started, begin with any of the following passages: Joshua 1:6–9; Psalm 23:1–6; 34:1–22; 56:9–13; Philippians 4:4–9; Matthew 6:25–34.[1]

---

[1] You should consult a mental health professional if you have chronic anxiety.

Growth, Gardens, & Grace

Day 5
Sticks and Stones

I have a chronic illness called "foot in mouth disease." Whatever thought pops into my head typically comes out of my mouth. Over the years, I have spent considerable effort learning to season my words with grace and hold my tongue.

Have you ever heard the children's saying "Sticks and stones may break my bones, but words will never hurt me"? Sadly, we know this aphorism simply isn't true. The author of Proverbs cautions that "The tongue can bring death or life," (Proverbs 18:21a). James warns that "the tongue is a flame of fire. It is a whole world of wickedness, corrupting your entire body. It can set your whole life on fire, for it is set on fire by hell itself," (James 3:6). Clearly, the authors of Scripture are trying to communicate that our words have a very real impact.

A friend of mine, Kira, gave me permission to share an experience from her past that fittingly illustrates the impact words can have. When Kira and her husband were dating, they decided to spend the day riding dirt bikes and ATVs with friends. Wanting to impress, Kira impulsively jumped onto a dirt bike despite having no idea how to drive it. The bike shot forward with Kira holding on for dear life. She quickly concluded the ride by crashing into a tree. Kira's legs were burned from top to bottom from the scorching motor, and cuts and bruises covered her body. Many years later, all the burns, cuts, and bruises have healed, but she still wears the scars that remind her of the impulsive decision.

In a similar way, when we speak before we think, our words can have a lasting impact on the people around us. In the verse above, James says that words can turn the course of someone's whole life "into a blazing flame of destruction and disaster!" Our words can create permanent damage by impacting the way someone thinks and feels.

The good news is that our words can also be used to make a positive impact on the people in our lives. Instead of destruction and disaster, our words can foster healing and joy. Proverbs 16:24 explains, "Kind words are like honey—sweet to the soul and healthy for the body." In Ephesians 4:29, Paul instructs, "Don't use foul or abusive language. Let everything you say be good and helpful, so that your words will be an encouragement to those who hear them."

Instead of harming others, our words can foster healing, joy, and encouragement. Speech seasoned with grace can even create a chain reaction that inspires people to spread love and kindness. We have an amazing opportunity to create positive change simply with our words! Let's share words that produce healing rather than scars.

Lord, thank you for teaching me about the impact of spoken words. I repent of using speech to wound my peers and loved ones. Help me think before I speak and only offer words that bring healing, joy, and encouragement. I pray that my words would lead others to you and cause them to take hold of the abundant life that you offer. In Jesus' name, Amen.

Personal Reflection

Meditate on your patterns of speech. Do your words ever tear others down rather than building them up? Do you honor God by speaking words that foster encouragement and healing? Be intentional about your speech today and ask God to help you honor Him and edify others.

Day 5

Day 6
City Park

New Orleans is my home away from home, as I completed my graduate degrees there. One of my favorite spots in NOLA is City Park, which is a full-on sensory experience. The massive live oaks create a serene, shady canopy. Curtains of Spanish moss hang from the thick branches and sway in the breeze. If you stop by Café DuMonde, you can sip rich café au lait and eat sweet beignets with mounds of powdered sugar. While you snack, you can sit on the shady patio, enjoy live jazz, and gaze at the mossy pond. If you walk across the "Great Lawn," you can sit on a porch swing beneath a trellis dripping with jasmine. If you are there during spring, the fragrance of the blooms is heavenly. Accompanying the sights and scents, burbling water fountains provide an audible backdrop for the peaceful setting.

Just thinking about the atmosphere of City Park in spring makes me feel serene. You and I, creatures who bear the image of God, take joy in beauty. We are inspired by spaces that are lovely. Throughout Scripture, cleanliness, orderliness, and beauty are traits worthy of admiration.

In the OT, God gave detailed instructions for the construction of the tabernacle and temple. The Father designed the holy edifice to reflect his glory and inspire his people. Every element represented something about God and his character. Thus, God called for fine fabrics of blue, purple, and crimson (Exodus 26:1) in addition to

Day 6

sculpted lilies, palm trees, pomegranates, and lions (1 Kings 7). Worshippers were inspired to draw near to God when they encountered the beauty and order of the sacred space.

As believers who have accepted Christ and received the gift of the Holy Spirit, sacred space now exists in and around us. Although we aren't commanded to keep our environment tidy or lovely, I believe that we more readily experience God's presence in spaces that reflect his character. Jesus implies that when our hearts are pure, our external space reflects the internal order. He says to the Pharisees, "First wash the inside of the cup and the dish, and then the outside will become clean, too," (Matthew 23:26).

Although the purity of our inner self is more important than our external environment, God knows that we thrive in uplifting spaces. He knows that if we're surrounded by garbage, we are more likely to feel like garbage. If our surroundings are chaotic, our thoughts will likely be chaotic. Our Father wants us to live joyfully, peacefully, and purposefully. Let's create spaces that inspire!

Lord, thank you for creating a beautiful world for me to inhabit and enjoy. Guide me as I seek to create physical spaces that promote joy and peace in my life. More importantly, help me live a life of purity so that my heart is clean. I pray that my life would inspire others to seek your presence. In Jesus' name, Amen.

Personal Reflection

Spend time making your environment more inspiring today. You can tidy up your workspace/home, play encouraging music, light a scented candle, add inspiring decor, or tackle an aesthetic project that brings you joy.

Growth, Gardens, & Grace

Day 7
Savor the Scent

Yesterday we discussed our immediate environment, and I described New Orleans City Park, a place that uplifts and inspires me. More specifically, one of my favorite aspects of City Park is the scent of spring in the air. The heavenly fragrance emanating from the park's flora offers welcome relief from the less appealing smells of the large city.

I've already mentioned the trellis dripping with jasmine in the central green. The fragrant flowers also bloom liberally upon fences, hedges, and anywhere else the vines can gain purchase. Throughout the park, the scent hangs in the air even when you can't see the jasmine. The small white flowers on the vine emit an aroma disproportionate to their tiny size. The scent is so encompassing that I feel as though I'm wrapped in a fragrant blanket.

The pervasive aroma of jasmine reminds me of God's presence. Just as the fragrance envelopes me, the presence of God surrounds us. Just as I smell the jasmine even when I can't see it, we experience his invisible presence. Alternatively, even when the fragrance is carried away by the wind, I know the jasmine vines still surround me. Likewise, even when we can't sense the presence of God, we can still be certain he is with us.

In Psalm 139, David meditates on God's presence.

> *O Lord, you have examined my heart*
> *and know everything about me.*

You know when I sit down or stand up.
You know my thoughts even when I'm far away.
You see me when I travel
and when I rest at home.
You know everything I do.
You know what I am going to say
even before I say it, Lord.
You go before me and follow me.
You place your hand of blessing on my head.
Such knowledge is too wonderful for me,
too great for me to understand!
I can never escape from your Spirit!
I can never get away from your presence!
If I go up to heaven, you are there;
if I go down to the grave, you are there.
If I ride the wings of the morning,
if I dwell by the farthest oceans,
even there your hand will guide me,
and your strength will support me.
I could ask the darkness to hide me
and the light around me to become night—
but even in darkness I cannot hide from you.
To you the night shines as bright as day.
Darkness and light are the same to you.

Psalm 139:1–12

Not only does God's presence surround us, but his presence dwells within us, goes before us, and follows behind us. He sees our thoughts, knows our motives, and protects our hearts.

Day 7

As the psalm progresses, David's tone shifts from exultant to wary. He rightly recognizes that God's constant presence is a cause for both celebration and caution. God enfolds us within his protection every moment of our lives. He sees every selfless act and kind word as well as every dishonorable thought and sinful action. We'll talk more about God's response to our sin later, but for now, let's focus on his presence.

God has blessed us with a beautiful planet that reflects his radiant glory and reminds us he is near. As we acknowledge his presence and abide in his care, we're empowered to serve him effectively and live with joy.

Heavenly Father, thank you for surrounding me with your presence. Thank you for going before me and for guarding my back. Thank you for being with me even when I don't feel your presence or deserve your grace. Forgive me for treating your presence lightly and disregarding your holiness. Help me live in obedience so that my sin doesn't hamper my relationship with you and prevent me from abiding in your presence. Help me to foster an atmosphere of peace and joy in my life so that I can better serve you and accomplish your will. I pray that I would be so immersed in your presence that others would experience your love through me. In Jesus' name, Amen.

Personal Reflection

Slowly re-read the passage above and meditate on David's words. Notice the thoughts and feelings that each verse evokes. Thank God for his constant care and protection, and give Him permission to point out any thoughts or behaviors that are dishonoring to his presence. Repent if needed, thank him for his loving guidance, and ask him to help you dwell in his presence more fully. You may want to write down a few notes because we'll refer back to this topic in a couple of weeks.

Growth, Gardens, & Grace

Day 8
State of Mind

Yesterday we talked about sensing the presence of God in spaces that are uplifting and inspiring. God knows that our external surroundings can influence our inner wellness. Likewise, our state of mind can impact the condition of our external surroundings. When we're depressed, we don't feel like dressing up or tidying up. When we're overwhelmed, we lack the physical and mental energy to create inspiring spaces and uplifting environments. Simply getting through each day seems like more than we can manage. Unfortunately, a dirty, dreary environment only exacerbates our mental struggle.[2]

So, how can we prevent our internal and external atmospheres from creating a downward spiral of dejection? Paul offers advice that can reverse the spiral or prevent it from occurring. He tells the Philippian church, "And now, dear brothers and sisters, one final thing. Fix your thoughts on what is true, and honorable, and right, and pure, and lovely, and admirable. Think about things that are excellent and worthy of praise," (Philippians 4:8). Paul exhorts each of us to make a decisive effort to create healthy patterns of thought. We must learn how to break the cycle of anxiety, stress, worry, and self-loathing. We must discipline ourselves to reject thoughts that dishonor God and

---

[2] Depression and anxiety can be caused by physiological factors. If you struggle with mental or emotional health, you should seek guidance from a mental health professional.

tempt us to sin. We must overcome critical, hateful, and angry inclinations, whether they are directed toward ourselves or others.

Just as exercise makes our physical body stronger, the more we take control of our thought life, the easier it gets. We can get a head start on improving our mental atmosphere by eliminating sources of negativity and vice. Refuse to watch shows and movies that promote violence and promiscuity. Don't listen to music that debases fellow humans, glorifies greed, or spews anger. Avoid gatherings in which you'll be tempted to compromise your faith. Redirect conversations involving gossip or slander.

Fortunately, the Holy Spirit empowers us to overcome an unhealthy mindset and replace it with the peace of God. He empowers us to cultivate healthy habits and patterns of thought. Each time we catch ourselves indulging a thought that doesn't honor God and foster joy, we can ask the Spirit to help us replace it with one that is true, honorable, right, pure, lovely, admirable, excellent, or praiseworthy.

God knows that we thrive in uplifting spaces, both internal and external. If we allow our minds to dwell on unpleasant thoughts or deteriorate into negativity, we lose the joy of the Lord. Let's cultivate both inner and outer spaces that produce an upward spiral of joy rather than a downward spiral of despair. Our Father wants us to live joyfully, serve fruitfully, and walk in the power of the Holy Spirit. Let's create spaces that inspire!

Heavenly Father, thank you for teaching me how to foster a healthy thought life. Give me the discipline to replace impure patterns of thought with those which are lovely and true. Forgive me for indulging in impure or unkind thoughts that draw me away from you. Give me the strength and diligence to reject influences that would negatively impact my mind. Bring thoughts to my mind that are true, honorable, right, pure, lovely, admirable, excellent, and praiseworthy. I pray that my mindset would be so healthy

Day 8

that my external surroundings reflect joy and peace. I pray that the joyful and peaceful atmosphere of my life would encourage others and inspire them to follow you. In Jesus' name, Amen.

Personal Reflection

Take a mental inventory, and prayerfully consider your own patterns of thought. Do you tend to think about things that are true, lovely, and encouraging or do you allow worry, resentment, or anger to dominate your mind? Do you focus on things that are pure, honorable, and praiseworthy or do you allow sin and temptation to govern your thoughts? As you go throughout your day, pay special attention to your thoughts and begin fostering a healthier mental atmosphere.

_____

_____

_____

_____

_____

_____

_____

_____

_____

_____

Day 9
Oasis — Part 1

The last few days, we've been talking about cultivating spaces that are inspiring, peaceful, and calming. We also discussed the negative feedback loop that can occur when our internal or external environment is disordered. Today, we'll talk about finding an oasis in which we can seek the presence of God, even when our lives are characterized by chaos or stress.

If you tend to be very logical or pragmatic, you may think that creating uplifting environments is a waste of time. Maybe you've surmised that you can feel peaceful and connect with God anywhere. Actually, though, we all need spaces that provide respite from the chaos of our busy lives.

As we discussed, City Park is a space that is beautiful and peaceful—a refreshing oasis amidst the bustling cityscape. The park is situated in the middle of New Orleans, a city packed with people, industry, and entertainment. The environment is almost always chaotic and loud, and as much as I love NOLA, parts of the city are smelly and dirty.

Like the frenetic pace of a big city, our lives can be chaotic and overwhelming. Mental overload and stress can make us feel like we're wandering in a desert wilderness. Like a dehydrated traveler shuffling through hot sand under a blazing sun, we slog through each day, putting one foot in front of the other, yet longing for relief. Like Israel wandering through the wilderness seeking the land of milk and honey, our souls long for a place of nourishment. However, we don't have to

Day 9

remain lost and stranded in the desert. The prophet Isaiah speaks directly to the weary traveler, exhorting us to seek refuge in our faith.

> *Have you never heard?*
> *Have you never understood?*
> *The Lord is the everlasting God,*
> *the Creator of all the earth.*
> *He never grows weak or weary.*
> *No one can measure the depths of his understanding.*
> *He gives power to the weak*
> *and strength to the powerless.*
> *Even youths will become weak and tired,*
> *and young men will fall in exhaustion.*
> *But those who trust in the Lord will find new strength.*
> *They will soar high on wings like eagles.*
> *They will run and not grow weary.*
> *They will walk and not faint.*
> **Isaiah 40:28–31**

Because our Father never grows weary, he can provide an endless supply of nourishment and strength for our souls. However, we must cultivate places and spaces of refuge in which we can access his refreshing and sustaining presence.

Although we always have access to the Spirit of God, identifying a physical space to which we can come when we need refreshing helps us more readily experience his presence and "hear" his voice. Removing ourselves, even momentarily, from the busyness of life is akin to turning down the volume on the world so we can hear the voice of our Father. Even better, spending time in our peaceful oasis with the Lord helps us abide in his presence more fully even when we return to the harsher environs of our lives. Let's slow down, seek God, and allow the Father to nourish our souls today.

Father, thank you for the gift of your Spirit, who refreshes my soul. Grow my desire to spend time in your presence. Teach me to prioritize time with you even when life seems too busy to take time away from my to-do list. I acknowledge that the most stressful and busy seasons of life are the times when I need you the most. Guide me as I seek to cultivate internal and external environments that enable me to draw closer to your presence and hear your voice more clearly. Open my eyes to places and spaces in my daily life to which I can retreat when my soul needs nourishment. In Jesus' name, Amen.

Personal Reflection

Take a few moments to declutter your internal and external space. Cultivate an atmosphere that draws you nearer to the presence of God, and thank him for nourishing your soul. Prayerfully create a list of uplifting activities and places to which you can escape when you need refreshing.

_____

_____

_____

_____

_____

_____

_____

Day 9

Day 10
Oasis — Part 2

Yesterday, we discussed the importance of seeking refuge in God's presence. Just as City Park is an oasis in the middle of New Orleans, we can create places of refuge in our lives. As we cultivate intentional moments and physical spaces with the Father, our weary souls are refreshed. As we seek refuge from the frenetic pace of life, we more clearly sense his love and guidance. As we turn down the volume of the world, we can better "hear" the voice of our Father.

When we routinely seek the oasis of God's presence in moments of solitude and quietude, the desert wilderness of our souls begins to transform. Instead of shuffling through hot sand with parched throats and weary legs, we begin to walk confidently in health, strength, and joy. As we abide in his nourishing love, God causes our personal refuge to grow and expand.

The Psalmist praises God for transforming the desert into a land of nourishment and fertility.

> *But he also turns deserts into pools of water,*
> *the dry land into springs of water.*
> *He brings the hungry to settle there*
> *and to build their cities.*
> *They sow their fields, plant their vineyards,*
> *and harvest their bumper crops.*
> *How he blesses them!*
> *They raise large families there,*

Day 10

> ### *and their herds of livestock increase.*
> ### ***Psalm 107:35–38***

As we cultivate places of physical, mental, and spiritual oasis in our own life, we become a refuge for others who are wandering in the desert.

Even Jesus took time to seek the presence of the Father. Matthew records that after feeding the 5,000, "Jesus insisted that his disciples get back into the boat and cross to the other side of the lake, while he sent the people home. After sending them home, he went up into the hills by himself to pray. Night fell while he was there alone," (Matthew 14:22–23). The Savior sent his disciples away from the bustling crowds, then sought solitude for himself. He knew that his capacity to serve others and fulfill his purpose was dependent upon his connection with the Father. The same held true for Jesus' disciples and still holds true for you and I.

Jesus came to earth with the most important mission in the history of the world. If he can make time for solitude with God, so can we. If the Savior found value in quiet time alone with the Father, we will certainly benefit from intimacy with God. Just as Jesus was intentional about seeking quietude and solitude, we must prioritize time with our Father—not just for our own benefit, but so we can share his peace, joy, and strength with those we love and with the people he has called us to serve.

Lord, thank you for being an oasis in the midst of a world that is often chaotic and harsh. Thank you for refreshing and nourishing my soul. Help me be diligent and intentional about spending distraction-free time with you. As I draw nearer to you, allow me to be a refuge for the people in my life. I pray that the joyful and peaceful atmosphere of my life would encourage others to accept the love of Christ. In Jesus' name, Amen.

Personal Reflection

Prayerfully evaluate your attitude toward time with God. Do you prioritize daily time with God or do you spend time with God only when you have an extra moment to spare? Do you view time with God as an interruption in your busy schedule or a means of equipping you to navigate life successfully? Do you have faith that your time with God is a vital investment in your soul, or do you doubt that you will get all your work done if you pause to seek God? Ask your Father to adjust any misaligned thinking or attitudes. If you don't already have a daily time of solitude with God, schedule intentional time with your Father every day for *at least* one week with a goal of making the time permanent.

_____

_____

_____

_____

_____

_____

_____

_____

_____

_____

_____

Day 11
Godly Grief

A few days ago, we discussed abiding in the presence of God in conjunction with Psalm 139. I pointed out that as the psalm progresses, David's tone shifts from joyful to cautious as he recognizes that God's constant attention is a cause for both celebration and fear. While God is attentive to our every need, he is also aware of every misguided thought, motive, and action. Although an awareness of his presence shouldn't cause shame or guilt, it should foster a healthy fear of the Lord, in which we seek to honor him by living in holiness.

Even though we fail time and time again, our Father knows we aren't perfect, and he loves us just the same. However, the Lord will often allow us to face the consequences of our own sin. Sadly, both the sin and our consequence grieve the heart of our Father.

In Hosea 11, God mourns over the disloyalty of his children and laments over their destruction.

> *When Israel was a child, I loved him,*
> *and I called my son out of Egypt.*
> *But the more I called to him,*
> *the farther he moved from me,*
> *offering sacrifices to the images of Baal*
> *and burning incense to idols.*
> *I myself taught Israel how to walk,*
> *leading him along by the hand.*

> *But he doesn't know or even care*
> *that it was I who took care of him.*
> *I led Israel along*
> *with my ropes of kindness and love.*
> *I lifted the yoke from his neck,*
> *and I myself stooped to feed him.*
> *But since my people refuse to return to me,*
> *they will return to Egypt*
> *and will be forced to serve Assyria.*
> *War will swirl through their cities;*
> *their enemies will crash through their gates.*
> *They will destroy them,*
> *trapping them in their own evil plans.*
> *For my people are determined to desert me.*
> *They call me the Most High,*
> *but they don't truly honor me.*
> *Oh, how can I give you up, Israel?*
> *How can I let you go?*
> *How can I destroy you like Admah*
> *or demolish you like Zeboiim?*
> *My heart is torn within me,*
> *and my compassion overflows.*
> ### *Hosea 11:1–8*

God shepherded Israel and tried to teach them how to live securely in the land as his people. He would have protected them and made them a light to the nations, but they rejected his guidance and love.

The Father was so grieved by the sin, suffering, and separation of his people, that he took decisive action on their behalf and ours. Since the consequences of sin could only be executed upon the

Day 11

perpetrators—humans—God became a human and endured the punishment that we deserved, i.e., death. Even better, our Savior defeated death so that God's children could experience eternal life and never again be separated from the Father. We simply cannot fathom the depth of God's love. What we can do, though, is love our Lord in return and express it through our holiness, service, and obedience (John 14:21).

Lord, thank you for taking the consequences of my sin so that I could experience unconditional love, abundant life, and eternity in your presence. Forgive me for stubbornly going my own way and rejecting your guidance. As I abide in your presence, I pray that any thoughts, motives, or behaviors that dishonor you would become repulsive to me. Help me see you for who you are—a loving Father rather than an angry dictator. Give me a desire to serve and obey you out of my own love for you as well as my gratitude for your sacrifice. In Jesus' name, Amen.

Personal Reflection

Our conception of God is shaped by many factors—family, religious background (or lack thereof), culture, and especially our experiences with male authority figures. Because the factors that shape our perception of God are flawed, our conceptions of him are likewise distorted. Prayerfully evaluate your own conception of the Father. Do you view him as an angry tyrant or a loving Father? Do you view Jesus as the embodiment of the Father, or do you view God as a harsh patriarch while Jesus is a beloved friend? Write down any thoughts or feelings about your Father that might reflect a distortion of his true character. Then cross out your wrong beliefs and write the truth in their place. If you struggle to complete the exercise, ask a trusted friend or mentor to help you.

Day 12
Pops

I mentioned in an Autumn devotional that I was close to my grandparents. Since my father passed away before I was born, my Pops took the role upon himself and raised me like his own daughter. As he had lost his own father at a young age, we shared a special bond. In fact, the first word I ever spoke was "Pops."

Born in 1925, Pops was of the generation in which kids had to be tough. He expected the same of his children and grandchildren. The fact that all of us—two daughters and four granddaughters—were girls didn't change his perspective. He raised us to be tough, resilient, and self-sufficient. He was more vested in teaching us to work hard than to act like ladies.

Pops's mother had provided for their family after his father died in a manufacturing accident. Although he never explicitly said so, I'm sure that watching both her struggle and her strength informed the way he raised his girls.

He expected hard work, high standards, and zero excuses. He forgave mistakes, but he expected us to admit when we made them. Pops loved to laugh, but he had a low tolerance for nonsense. Not surprisingly, I exceeded his nonsense tolerance on more than a few occasions.

On one family visit to Kentucky when I was around five, I was being exceptionally sassy. After numerous warnings, Pops decided that disciplinary measures were required. He took me aside to speak privately, knelt down, and explained that he was going to discipline me for my poor behavior. He then proceeded to place me over his knee and spank me.

A spanking from my Pops was rare and the discipline hurt my heart more than my behind. I was utterly humiliated, but I knew the discipline was justified. I knew Pops would tolerate nothing less than my best. Not for a moment did I doubt his love.

Our Heavenly Father likewise calls his children to a high standard. The author of Proverbs 3 exhorts, "My child, don't reject the Lord's discipline, and don't be upset when he corrects you. For the Lord corrects those he loves, just as a father corrects a child in whom he delights," (Proverbs 3:11–12). Although our Father doesn't discipline us for every mistake, he often takes measures to correct repeated patterns of unhealthy behavior. He knows that when we engage in willful and persistent sin, we hurt ourselves and the people around us.

God's discipline can take various forms. Sometimes God sends correction through words of rebuke from a loved one or trusted friend. Sometimes he allows us to face the consequences of our actions so we can learn from our mistakes. Sometimes he allows us to face a completely unrelated trial to draw us back into his arms.

Discipline is never pleasant, but the outcome is worthwhile. Paul reminds us that, "No discipline is enjoyable while it is happening—it's painful! But afterward there will be a peaceful harvest of right living for those who are trained in this way," (Hebrews 12:11).

The correction I received from Pops chafed against my free spirit and strong will until he passed away when I was in my early twenties. Back then, I didn't appreciate his chastisement, but I now understand that he was instilling valuable life lessons and preparing me to succeed at life. I hope we can all lean into the loving correction of our Heavenly Father and reap the benefits of his attentive care.

Day 12

Father, thank you for your hand of discipline in my life. Help me to turn from every behavior that dishonors you and damages my soul. Give me a desire to live according to your standards. Teach me to accept correction rather than making excuses. Instill in me the humility to learn from my mistakes. Help me also discern between healthy correction and hurtful criticism from other people. Show me how to abide fully in your love while maintaining respect for your holy standards. In Jesus' name, Amen.

Personal Reflection

Recall several instances in the past in which you faced valid discipline or correction. Were you able to learn and grow from your experiences or did you reject the feedback you received? Prayerfully consider how you can respond more productively in the future.

_____

_____

_____

_____

_____

_____

_____

_____

_____

_____

Day 13
Gone Fishin'

My Pops worked hard, but he also played hard. Times with him and my Gram are among the most treasured moments of my childhood. I especially loved to go fishing with Pops.

One of our earliest outings, however, took an unexpected turn. We'd enjoyed a lovely morning on the river in Pops' fishing boat. As we approached the shallows to dock the boat, I leaned over the side and tumbled right into the water. (I was clumsy then, and I'm still quite clumsy now.) We were close enough to shore that I was able to crawl out without panic. The greater problem was that I was soaking wet with no towel or dry clothing. We were also a substantial drive from home.

Always prepared, Pops searched his truck for options. I distinctly remember him pulling a ratty old set of long johns from behind the truck seat. Although they were a million sizes too big, I was thrilled to put on the wrinkled garments. I was honored to wear clothing that belonged to my Pops.

Our Heavenly Father likewise clothes us in his garments. Paul explains, "For you are all children of God through faith in Christ Jesus. So, all of you who were washed in Christ have clothed yourselves in Christ," (Galatians 3:26–27, my translation). When we accept the lordship of Christ, we take off our dirty, soggy, old clothing and put on the garments of our Savior and his Father. Instead of wrinkled long johns, our new garments consist of righteousness, love, forgiveness, and humility. They're the royal vestment of a king!

Like Pops' long johns, the garments of our Heavenly Father can be ill-fitting initially. Although we are honored to wear them, they might seem like big ideals and high standards into which we'll never grow. As we mature however, we begin to fill out our new clothing. Eventually, we grow into his garments so well that we never take them off, at least not intentionally.

Although I never wore Pop's long johns again, I hope you'll clothe yourself in Christ daily. Let's wear the garments of our Father with pride and show them off at every opportunity!

Father, thank you for clothing me with righteousness, love, forgiveness, and humility. Refine areas of my life in which your clothing chafes. Help me to grow into your garments as I grow in spiritual maturity. Empower me to wear your vestment with pride as a declaration of my allegiance with and obedience to you. In Jesus' name, Amen.

Personal Reflection

Prayerfully reflect on your attitude toward wearing the garments of your Father. Do you keep them shoved away, only taking them out when you go to church? Do you wear them only when you need your Father to clean you up after falling into a muddy swamp? Do you try to wear them at all times, but catch yourself peeling them off when they become uncomfortable? Do you don them with pride and willingly conform yourself to the garments he has provided. Pray for God to show you at least one area of your spiritual life in which you can better grow into the garments of your Father.

Day 13

Day 14
I Caught a Moss!

Yesterday we discussed my unfortunate stumble into the river while fishing with Pops. Another fishing trip stands out prominently in my recollection as well. The memory is vivid because I was overjoyed at my unconventional catch.

I was just learning to fish and was delighted to catch anything at all. So, when I felt tension on my line, I began to reel in my quarry with great vehemence. I employed all the strength my little arms could muster to draw my catch closer to the boat.

The moment a catch emerges from the water is exciting for every fisherman (or fisherwoman). It's like unwrapping a wet, stinky birthday present that you can boast about to your friends. Thus, I reeled my catch above the water with great anticipation. I was delighted to see a gooey green clump and questioningly looked to Pops for an explanation. With a chuckle, he revealed that I had snared a patch of moss. So, with glee, I lifted my dripping prey further into the air and declared, "I caught a moss!"

My delight over catching the messy goo was a source of endless amusement for Pops, who shared the anecdote at every opportunity. I didn't mind, since I loved to be the center of his attention and the subject of his conversations. Yet, Pops did more than chuckle at my misplaced enthusiasm. He taught me how to be a real fisherman. He taught me how to tell the difference between clumps of junk and actual fish. He taught me how to bait hooks and remove fish from hooks

Day 14

once I'd caught them. As I grew older, we transitioned from the river to the ocean, going deep sea fishing on numerous occasions. Instead of little rods and reels with bobbers, I learned to utilize heavy duty tackle. Instead of cute little river fishies, I transitioned to catching fish the size of my little sister. I learned to wear a harness, brace my feet, and use my entire body to best the massive ocean dwellers.

My point is that Pops made sure I progressed beyond catching moss. We fished together for many years, and he taught me the skills I needed. Jesus similarly spent time with his disciples, teaching them over a period of years. Mark 1:16–18 records the moment Jesus called Simon Peter and Andrew to follow him.

> *One day as Jesus was walking along the shore of the Sea of Galilee, he saw Simon and his brother Andrew throwing a net into the water, for they fished for a living. Jesus called out to them, "Come, follow me, and I will show you how to fish for people!" And they left their nets at once and followed him. A little farther up the shore Jesus saw Zebedee's sons, James and John, in a boat repairing their nets. He called them at once, and they also followed him, leaving their father, Zebedee, in the boat with the hired men.*
>
> *Mark 1:16–18*

Jesus called his disciples to become fishers of men instead of fishers of . . . well, fish. He walked with them, talked with them, and taught them one lesson at a time.

Just as Jesus equipped his disciples day by day, he equips you and I to grow at the pace we need. Jesus wants to teach us, guide us, and celebrate each victory. However, we must spend time with him to learn from him. If I'd never gone fishing with Pops, I would never have learned to fish. In addition, just like Pops celebrating my moss,

Jesus is pleased with even small steps of growth. He celebrates our success, then gently guides us toward greater steps of faith. He is never impatient, and he loves spending time with us. Let's go fishing with Jesus today!

Lord, thank you for helping me grow, step by step. Give me a desire to spend time in your presence so that I can learn how to build your kingdom and become an effective fisher of men. Grow my capacity to learn from you and sense the guidance of your Spirit. Help me recognize even small steps of growth and learn to celebrate them. Teach me greater humility and patience so that I remain content as I grow into the purpose for which you've called me. In Jesus' name, Amen.

Personal Reflection

What seemingly insignificant progress can you celebrate today? What small victories might make your Father proud? As you navigate your day, be intentional about celebrating moments of personal and spiritual growth.

_____

_____

_____

_____

_____

_____

_____

_____

Day 14

Day 15
Small Starts

Yesterday we discussed the process of growth that takes place as we become fully devoted disciples of Christ. Just as I began my fishing career by catching moss, we all start small and gradually grow to maturity.

The Jewish people faced their own small start upon returning to the land after Babylon had invaded Judea, razed Jerusalem, and deported the population. Once Babylon had fallen to the Persians, however, their new overlords allowed the Jewish people to return and rebuild. The process was slow and tumultuous, but God encouraged his people through the prophets. He gave Zechariah a message specifically for Zerubbabel, the leader of the returning exiles.

> Then he said to [Zechariah], "This is what the Lord says to Zerubbabel: It is not by force nor by strength, but by my Spirit, says the Lord of Heaven's Armies. Nothing, not even a mighty mountain, will stand in Zerubbabel's way; it will become a level plain before him! And when Zerubbabel sets the final stone of the Temple in place, the people will shout: 'May God bless it! May God bless it!' . . . Zerubbabel is the one who laid the foundation of this Temple, and he will complete it. Then you will know that the Lord of Heaven's Armies has sent me. Do not despise these

Day 15

> *small beginnings, for the Lord rejoices to see the work begin, to see the plumb line in Zerubbabel's hand."*
> ***Zechariah 4:6–7, 9–10***

The people of Judah possessed scarce resources and faced opposition on every side, but God reminded them that he was the source of their strength. Material wealth and military might wouldn't bring restoration and growth. Only God could do that.

The success of the Jewish people wouldn't come automatically though. Even as they depended upon the Lord for provision, they would have to work diligently. According to Zechariah, the Lord "rejoices to see the work begin [and] to see the plumb line in Zerubbabel's hand." In case you aren't familiar, a plumb line is a builder's tool for establishing straight vertical planes. (I had to look it up myself a few years ago.) In other words, God expected each citizen, from the smallest to the greatest, to get to work!

In regard to my own growth and that of my Pops, small beginnings were no impediment for God. I've already mentioned that Pops grew up in the depression, dirt poor, with no father to provide for their family. With only a high school education, he rose to a key supervisory position in a large chemical plant. He provided well for his family and his girls lacked nothing.

My own life, likewise, began in adversity, with the death of my father, and soon after, an abusive step-father (not my current step-dad, he's awesome). Yet, thanks to the Lord, a courageous and hardworking mom, a new step-dad who loved me like his own, and a Pops who taught me everything I needed to know about life, God equipped me to reach my dreams and even surpass them.

Our small beginnings aren't a hindrance to our Father, they are an opportunity for his glory to shine. In fact, Paul reminds us that God's power is perfected in our weaknesses (2 Corinthians 12:19).

God owns all the resources and holds limitless power. Even better, he loves to bless his children. What small starts can you celebrate today?

Lord, thank you for equipping me with the tools I need to succeed in life. Thank you for providing all the resources I need to walk according to your plans. Teach me to lean upon your love and follow your guidance. Grow my faith so that I obey your commands and pursue my goals with integrity rather than succumbing to the customs and temptations of the world. Guard my heart so that I don't seek success for my own benefit, but so that I can be a blessing to your Kingdom. I pray that you would be glorified by my small starts and continuing growth. In Jesus' name, Amen.

Personal Reflection

Prayerfully meditate on your personal growth trajectory. Are you feeling frustrated by any slow starts or small beginnings? Ask God to show you whether you simply need to trust him more or if you need to, like Zerubbabel, pick up the plumb line and get to work

_____

_____

_____

_____

_____

_____

_____

_____

Day 15

Day 16
Shoes of Shame

Over the last couple of days, we've discussed spiritual and personal growth. We'll talk more about growth as we continue through the spring. Today, however, I want to discuss integrity, a virtue that will either catalyze our growth or, if absent, bring our growth to a screeching halt. Allow me to illustrate with another fishing story.

First, let me explain that my Gram was a petite lady. Unlike Gram, I've never been petite. By the time I was ten years old, I could wear her clothes and shoes, which I often did. So, on one particular morning when Pops and I decided to go fishing, I happened to be wearing a pair of Gram's slip-on sneakers.

Before we departed, Gram warned Pops not to drive the boat fast. She knew that he enjoyed getting out on the river and letting it rip, but she didn't want him doing it with me in the boat. So, with assurances that we would drive safely and slowly, Pops and I headed out.

Once we were in the boat and on the water, I wanted to get comfortable. I slipped off my sneakers (i.e. Gram's sneakers), and settled into my seat. As we navigated toward deeper water, temptation got the best of Pops. He gassed the boat and we went flying. What would be the harm? Gram would never know, and I was delighted by the speed at which we raced over the water—that is, right up until Gram's shoes blew out of the boat. Pops quickly brought the boat to a stop and turned us around, but it was too late. The shoes were gone beneath the depths of the water.

Day 16

I wouldn't say that the incident ruined our trip, but I will say that we dreaded the stern reprimand we knew we would face when we got home.

My point is that our hidden transgressions always find their way out of hiding. We think our sins are safely tucked away in the dark, but the light always gets switched on somehow. Even when we think our skeletons are locked in the closet, they eventually saunter out the door.

Jesus warned of hidden sin during his time on this earth. He taught, "The time is coming when everything that is covered up will be revealed, and all that is secret will be made known to all. Whatever you have said in the dark will be heard in the light, and what you have whispered behind closed doors will be shouted from the housetops for all to hear!" (Luke 12:2–3). Although Jesus spoke about his final return when all people will stand before him, the principle is true for our present season of life as well.

If we simply live with integrity, we don't have to worry about getting caught or facing consequences. If we navigate life as Jesus recommends, we won't lose our metaphorical shoes. Additionally, our hidden sins always impact others. (I didn't just lose my own shoes—I lost Gram's!) The strain of our sin causes unnecessary friction in our life that harms our relationships and impedes our growth. Let's proactively avoid such obstacles and move full speed ahead into the growth that our Father wants for us!

Father, thank you for declaring me righteous and holy. Give me a desire to honor you and my loved ones by living honestly and transparently. Give me the courage to confess my hidden sins and obtain freedom from them. I pray that you would expose the root issues that have led me to disobey you. Create in me a clean heart and cultivate in me a desire to live with integrity. In Jesus' name, Amen.

Personal Reflection

Most of us hide at least 10% of our true selves from others. Prayerfully reflect and determine whether you are holding anything back from those closest to you. Ask God to give you the courage to confess any hidden sins so that you can receive healing and live with integrity.

Day 17
Back to the Future

Growing up, I spent every Saturday night with Gram and Pops. On the surface, our weekends would have appeared quite boring, but they were my favorite part of every week.

My grandparents enjoyed collecting antiques, with the hope of opening a small antique shop one day (which they did). So, each Saturday night we would attend an auction. Most of the auctions were in barns in varying stages of disrepair. The floors would be covered in gravel or dirt, and a cloud of tobacco smoke would hang in the air. We sat on hard wooden benches, or if we were lucky, metal folding chairs. Activities for kids were nonexistent, and iPhones didn't yet exist.

Nonetheless, I relished our outings. I loved that we were searching for hidden treasures and neglected items of overlooked value. I loved listening to the rhythmic staccato of the auctioneers. Once I grew tired of the proceedings, Gram would buy me a bag of popcorn and we would play tic-tac-toe on the small paper tablet she kept in her purse.

The best part of the night came after the auction. Once we got home, Gram would let me don one of her soft, pink, floor-length nighties. (Since she was tiny and I was tall for my age, it worked well.) If we had gotten home in time, we would watch the Golden Girls and various other Saturday night sitcoms. Finally, we would go to bed and talk about life until I fell asleep.

Growth, Gardens, & Grace

I didn't think Saturday could be any more perfect until, one night, we *didn't* go to an auction. As we left the house, Gram and Pops informed me that they had a surprise in store. We shortly arrived at the movie theater, and I watched as Pops purchased three tickets to *Back to the Future*. At the time, I was 7 years old, and going to the movie theater was a rare treat. I'd previously seen *Bambi*, which was both traumatic and enchanting, as well as *Indiana Jones and the Temple of Doom*, which was thrillingly frightening. So, going to the theater with Gram and Pops was better than an ice cream sundae with a cherry on top. Of course, the movie itself was so good that all the ingredients combined to create one of the best nights of my life.

Moments like my *Back to the Future* night don't occur very often. The tenor of most days is more akin to mundane moments sitting on a hard bench listening to a boring auction. Yet, we can choose to find joy in the mundane. In fact, we can choose joy even when life is worse than mundane. As I mentioned a couple of days ago, I had a tumultuous period in my childhood, and for me, those years were among the most difficult and frightening of my life.

Yet, I now realize that God provided a safe refuge through Gram and Pops. Despite various trials, my heart remained full of joy. In Psalm 30:10–11, David similarly praises God, "You have turned my mourning into joyful dancing. You have taken away my clothes of mourning and clothed me with joy, that I might sing praises to you and not be silent. O Lord my God, I will give you thanks forever!" And in Psalm 4:8, he declares, "In peace I will lie down and sleep, for you alone, O Lord, will keep me safe."

Whether we are in a season of trial or simply in the midst of the mundane, God offers a source of peace and joy. We can eagerly anticipate our next mountain-top movie night experience. Until then, however, we simply have to widen our field of vision to see his daily blessings. Perhaps we feel like we're sitting on an uncomfortable

Day 17

wooden bench, but perhaps we just need to look at the person sitting next to us. Perhaps we need to savor that bag of hot, salty popcorn. Perhaps we need to relish the silky soft nightie. Only you can savor the blessings and dwell in the refuge he has created for you. Let's count each blessing and give thanks for each one today!

Lord, thank you for being a refuge from which I can experience peace and joy. Open my eyes so that I see the blessings all around me. Help me savor every moment and dwell in your presence. Teach me to focus my gaze on you and your goodness instead of dwelling upon the mundane or undesirable aspects of life. Forgive me for failing to acknowledge your protection and provision. Grow the joy in my heart so that I can be a blessing and encouragement to those around me. In Jesus' name, Amen.

Personal Reflection

Make a list of mundane blessings below—people or things that are so familiar that you often forget to appreciate them. Thank God for each one, then open your eyes to look for more as you navigate your day.

_____

_____

_____

_____

_____

_____

_____

Day 18
Purple Hearts

Today we'll delve into topics that may be unsettling for sensitive souls. If you are hesitant to read about the trials of war, you may want to skip the following two paragraphs.

My Pops was definitely among those of the "Greatest Generation." In addition to facing the grisly manufacturing death of his father and helping his family survive the Great Depression, he fought valiantly in World War II. Pops fought in the Ardennes Offensive, otherwise known as the Battle of the Bulge. In case you aren't familiar, this battle was one of the most important of the entire war. Ardennes was the last major offensive attempted by the Axis powers. The surprise attack by Germany and her allies devastated the largely American forces holding the Belgian front. In fact, the Battle of the Bulge was the largest and bloodiest battle of the entire war, with nearly 90,000 casualties and 20,000 on the Allied forces alone. Yet, the valiant Allied soldiers held the line and defeated their attackers. Their crucial victory marked the beginning of the German retreat and, ultimately, the end of the war.

My Pops was among the 90,000 casualties, but thankfully not among the deaths. He was shot twice, once in the chest, a scant inch from his heart, and once in the hip, an injury from which he never fully recovered. He lay on the battlefield, among the other injured and dead, for an entire day before being rescued. He was awarded two Purple Hearts for his bravery. Nonetheless, the experience was one that caused such severe emotional (and physical) scarring that he would never talk about his experience. He simply had no desire to revisit the horrors he'd experienced.

This portrait of a man who survived unimaginable trauma and horror during the first twenty years of his life seems inconsistent with the Pops I knew and loved—the compassionate father who clothed me in his long johns and shared my joy at catching "a moss," the gentle gardener who grew roses, cucumbers, and tomatoes, the wise mentor who taught me to work hard, play hard, and relish every moment.

Although Pops wasn't especially "religious," I'm confident he knew and loved the Lord. In fact, he explicitly told me so. But more than that, his life proved it. Pops always had a laugh, a smile, and a hug for his girls. Everyone he met instantly felt comfortable in his presence; many people, even those outside the family, affectionately called him "Pops."

In short, he was full of the joy, kindness, and love of God. Yet, to say that the joy of the Lord was his strength is an oversimplification. He was privy to a secret that few people today seem to know: Pops learned to be content in any circumstance because his faith was rooted in Christ. As Paul teaches in Philippians,

> *Not that I was ever in need, for I have learned how to be content with whatever I have. I know how to live on almost nothing or with everything. I have learned the secret of living in every situation, whether it is with a full stomach or empty, with plenty or little. For I can do everything through Christ, who gives me strength.*
>
> ### *Philippians 4:11–13*

Pops' well-being was dependent upon Jesus rather than his circumstances. Life is full of ups and downs, good seasons and hard seasons. Pops knew that the down-swings wouldn't last forever, but neither would the up-swings. Therefore, he could walk with fortitude through any situation.

Sadly, Philippians 4:13 is often divorced from context. Many people, including myself, have used the verse in reference to personal victories, football games, and every manner of competition. However, the verse isn't about winning. Paul is teaching us to be content whether we win *or lose*! The apostle is encouraging us to root our faith in the eternal rather than the temporal because only then will we win the best prize—the peace and joy of Christ.

Lord, thank you for providing a safe and lasting refuge in which I can place my hope. Teach me to root my contentment in who you are rather than what is happening in my life. Help me grow in fortitude so that I'm not dismayed by setbacks. Forgive me for doubting you when trials crop up in my life. Fill my heart with such faith that depression and discontent have no ground in which they can take root. Grow my joy to the extent that others notice and I have opportunities to share the reason for my hope. In Jesus' name, Amen.

Personal Reflection

Prayerfully reflect on your personal fortitude. Can you navigate trials without sinking into depression or numbing your wounds with unhealthy strategies? Can you rebound without venting frustrations on those you love or attacking people who are trying to help you? Can you move on with your daily tasks or do you struggle to get out of bed in the morning? If you struggle with depression and anxiety, or if you struggle to recover from trials, consider seeing a professional counselor. Wherever you fall on the spectrum, however, ask God to show you a few opportunities for growth.

Day 19
A Handy Way to Pray

Yesterday we discussed my Pops' experience in WWII. Most of us have strong opinions about war and military operations. Yet, while our opinions are strong, our prayer efforts are typically weak. Regardless of our opinions, we are called and commanded to intercede for others. Paul instructs us to, "devote yourselves to prayer with an alert mind and thankful heart," (Colossians 4:2). Although Scripture doesn't specifically instruct us to pray for soldiers, we can make a powerful difference in the world through strategic prayer. In fact, when we intercede for others, we go to battle on their behalf.

But how can we pray powerfully and strategically when so many issues around the world need intercession? I would venture to say that we all pray for ourselves and for our families. Yet, praying for people and situations outside our immediate bubble can feel overwhelming. To help, I'd like to propose an organizational rubric for our daily prayer time. The format isn't intended to be restrictive or prohibitive, but rather to serve as a tool to facilitate a more potent prayer life.

I like to call the method "a handy way to pray" because we use our fingers to organize our prayer life. Each finger is assigned a particular day of the week and category. (Since we have 5 fingers per hand and 7 days per week, your prayers on the 2 extra days can take whatever form you want.) Starting with our thumb, the digit closest to our heart, we pray for ourselves and our immediate family. Next, the index finger reminds us to pray for close friends and extended family. As we proceed outward from our core relationships, the middle finger prompts us to pray for our faith family, workplace, schools, and community. The ring finger, then, reminds us to pray for our enemies—people with whom we disagree, people we are striving to forgive, and people we simply dislike. Finally, the pinky finger reminds us to pray for the armed forces, first responders, U.S. government, and world rulers.

Of course, we can customize and create our own "handy prayer." Simply remember that as we engage in warfare through prayer, "we are not fighting against flesh-and-blood enemies, but against evil rulers and authorities of the unseen world, against mighty powers in this dark world, and against evil spirits in the heavenly places," (Ephesians 6:12). As we pray for God to defend the righteous, let's also intercede for those who are enslaved to evil. As we pray for God to strengthen the hearts of those who love him, we can likewise pray for God to soften hearts too hardened to receive his love. As we go to battle on behalf of our loved ones and lost neighbors, we should also pray for the ultimate and permanent defeat of the Enemy. Let's echo the words of Jesus and pray, "May your Kingdom come soon. May your will be done on earth, as it is in heaven," (Matthew 6:10).

Father, thank you for empowering me to do battle on behalf of my loved ones through prayer. Grow my desire to intercede for my community, nation, and world. Convict my heart when I grow lax about praying for others. Open my eyes to the needs around me and soften my heart toward those with whom I disagree. Help me see others through your eyes and be moved to intercede for them. In Jesus' name, Amen.

Day 19

Personal Reflection

Take a moment to organize your own "handy prayer." If you like the model I suggested, use it! If you want to customize or rearrange, write your plan in the space provided. After you're finished, pray through the first of your five fingers today!

_____

_____

_____

_____

_____

_____

_____

_____

_____

_____

_____

_____

_____

Day 20
Flying Kites

I've never enjoyed flying kites. I begin each attempt with optimism as my kite soars into the sky only to watch my hopes crash to the ground along with my kite. If I'm being honest, I feel the same way about prayer at times. Although I know God hears me, my prayers sometimes seem to float upward toward God, hit turbulence in the atmosphere, then fall back down with a splat. Simply put, prayer has always been a struggle for me.

After years of self-analysis, I've identified several reasons for my struggle. First, I'm a control freak and I have trouble surrendering to God's sovereign, unknowable plan. Second, I'm addicted to accomplishing tasks, and prayer doesn't provide instant gratification. Third, I subconsciously feel like I'm not righteous enough for God to hear my prayers. I mean, James clearly tells us, "The earnest prayer of a righteous person has great power and produces wonderful results," (James 5:16b). How could I possibly be righteous enough to pray with great efficacy?

In reality, none of us are righteous enough to approach God in prayer, much less procure "wonderful results." We know from Paul's teaching that "No one is righteous—not even one," (Romans 3:10). Even the most holy person among us is filthy before God. That's why we need Jesus! When we accept him as Lord, the Savior declares each of us righteous. So, James is actually teaching that the prayers of every single Christ-follower are powerful. James 5:16 is not a statement

Day 20

about the proportional relationship between righteousness and effective prayer. It's a statement about the power of prayer! Your prayers are powerful because your God is powerful.

God always answers our prayers. Yet, his response isn't always in the manner we expect or in the timing we have planned. If we feel like God isn't responding to our prayers, we might need to broaden our frame of reference. Sometimes we become so focused on our own plan that we fail to see what God is actually doing. Our prayers haven't tumbled to the ground, they've simply soared beyond our perception. Unlike my unsuccessful and disappointing attempts at kite flying, our prayers produce results beyond our highest expectations.

Lord, thank you for hearing every prayer and responding with great wisdom and infinite knowledge. Help me trust you even when I don't see results in the timing or manner I expect. Help me grow in righteousness so that I can better understand how you are working in my life and my world. Teach me to desire your will more than my own, and give me a greater desire to spend time with you in prayer. In Jesus' name, Amen.

Personal Reflection

First, make a written or mental list of any needs for which you have been praying recently, especially situations in which your prayers have felt ineffective or unproductive. Pray over each need, asking God to align your heart with his and to reveal how he might be responding in an unexpected manner. Second, remember to pray through day 2 of your "handy prayer"!

_____

_____

Growth, Gardens, & Grace

Day 21
Farmer's Market

As we discussed yesterday, we often approach prayer with the wrong expectations and motives. Although God always answers our prayers, the means and timing of his response sometimes fails to meet our expectations. At times, we treat our Heavenly Father like a cosmic vending machine at which we become angry when our desired treats are not dispensed. What if, instead, we approached God as a loving Father and faithful friend? Allow me to illustrate.

Abel and I love to visit the farmer's market together. We enjoy browsing the stalls and walking our friendly dogs. We savor the scents of homemade candles and soaps. We sample organic snacks and freshly brewed coffee or lemonade. We sometimes purchase fresh produce or hand-crafted goods, but not always. In other words, going to the market isn't about getting stuff, it's about our time together.

As we browse, we chat about life. Sometimes our conversations are trivial and sometimes meaningful. We stay up-to-date on one another's likes and dislikes. We share the high points and the low points of our week. We discuss frustrating situations and upcoming celebrations.

In a similar manner, our prayer time shouldn't solely be about getting things from God. In prayer, we draw nearer to the heart of our Father. We share our hopes, dreams, fears, and failures. We intercede for the people in our life, and we allow him to align our hearts with his.

Prayer is about transformation, not personal gratification. That is why Jesus could honestly teach, "If you remain in me and my words remain in you, you may ask for anything you want, and it will be granted!" (John 15:7). As we mature in Christ, our hearts move into alignment with the heart of the Father. His will becomes our greatest desire as we seek the good of others and the growth of the kingdom. Of course, we still present our personal requests to him, and God desires that we do so, but our time with him can be so much more. If Abel simply asked me to buy him a list of groceries, which he often does, I certainly would. But if we never took time to slow down and walk through the market together, we would both miss out on meaningful and rich experiences together. We don't have to meander through the farmer's market every day, but setting aside regular time together deepens and strengthens our relationship in meaningful ways.

Father, thank you for being attentive to every prayer I pray. Forgive me for pelting you with demands instead of seeking time in your presence. Give me a desire to spend rich and meaningful time with you. Show me how to discern your will rather than trying to impose my own. Align my heart with yours, and show me how to abide in your love. Teach me how to be still in your presence and listen for your voice. In Jesus' name, Amen.

Personal Reflection

Spend time talking with God as if you were confiding in your closest friend. Instead of asking him for anything, simply share what is on your heart. How are you feeling and what are you thinking? What situations are bringing you joy or causing you frustration? As you pray, be sure to pause occasionally and listen for the still, small voice of God. Don't feel frustrated if you don't immediately sense a response. The more we practice listening, however, the better we'll hear him when he does respond. Before you conclude your prayer time today, remember to pray through day 3 of your "handy prayer"!

Day 21

Day 22
Love Thy Neighbors

I basically live on my back porch. In fact, most of these devotionals were written there. It's my little slice of heaven on earth. From my comfy patio chair, I can see the edge of my next door neighbors' yard, where Smokey's best schnauzer friend, Max, lives. I can gaze at the pond just down the hill and to the right. To my left, I can see our peaceful cul-de-sac around which more lovely neighbors live.

My immediate space is filled by floor-to-ceiling plants, a couple of small folding tables for writing (gifts from a neighbor), and an open space reserved for outdoor workouts. The scent of jasmine and basil fill the air during the spring and summer, while the buzz of hummingbirds fills my heart. Of course, my dogs are always by my side, usually napping on the cool patio floor or sunning in the warm grass. Even on the hottest days of summer, we'll recline beneath the shade of the overhead fan and listen to the breezy birdsong.

Lately, however, my haven for meditation, exercise, and writing has become somewhat less than peaceful. You see, a new family moved into our tranquil cul-de-sac. Shortly after their arrival, I realized that my outdoor sanctuary would never be quite the same.

The volume at which the new family communicated was anything but peaceful. Although I am a characteristically loud person, the decibel level was beyond anything I've experienced outside of a rock concert. I tried covering the sound with music and headphones, but my run-of-the-mill earbuds weren't up to the challenge. The noise was so

Day 23

loud that we could even sometimes hear the new family from inside our house.

Over the first few weeks, I made a couple of feeble attempts to chat with the mom and kids. Feeling that my gestures were unwelcome, however, I made no further attempts. I simply tried to move on with life, yet continued to experience extreme frustration each time my outdoor activities were interrupted by unwelcome noise. My standard response soon became gathering my supplies and retreating to my indoor office.

Eventually, though, the Holy Spirit convicted me about my bad attitude. Instead of being self-absorbed and selfish about my space, I should be praying for this young family. In fact, loving our neighbors and praying for them is a direct command in Scripture. We've all read the familiar words of Jesus, "You have heard the law that says, 'Love your neighbor' and hate your enemy. But I say, love your enemies! Pray for those who persecute you! In that way, you will be acting as true children of your Father in heaven," (Matthew 5:43–45). I realized that I had grossly failed to live out Jesus' words. These people were my literal neighbors, not my enemies. And even if they were my enemies, I would still be called to love them and pray for them.

Thus, I resolved to make a change. Whenever my peace was disrupted by neighborly noise, I would pray for them. Instead of getting mad, gathering my things, and going inside, I would intercede on their behalf. At that moment, the peaceful atmosphere of my porch began to return. Now, each time the cul-de-sac volume starts to rise, the amplitude of my prayer life rises with it.

Are any difficult people or situations disrupting your peace? You have the power to respond intentionally rather than reacting emotionally. You are the only person who has the capacity to control your inner peace. Instead of fleeing in frustration, rise to the challenge through the power of prayer. I must confess, I still haven't gotten the courage to build a relationship with my newest neighbors, but I've taken the first step. And, hey, we all have room to grow!

Lord, thank you for teaching me to love as you love. Help me see other people through your eyes and treat them with the kindness they deserve as your children. Teach me to respond with compassion rather than reacting with irritation in difficult situations. Change my heart so that my first response is prayer instead of anger. Empower me to extend grace whenever I am offended. In Jesus' name, Amen.

Personal Reflection

Pray through day 4 of your "handy prayer." Intercede on behalf of anyone who offends you, angers you, or frustrates you. Pray over any people or situations that are disrupting your peace. Finally, pray over any people you consider your enemy, and pray for God's help to love them.[3]

_____

_____

_____

_____

_____

_____

---

[3] If you are struggling with unforgiveness, I recommend reading or re-reading days 77–81 in *Home, Hope, & Holidays: Winter Devotionals Inspired by God's Creation*. For more in-depth reading see Tim Keller, *Forgive: Why Should I and How Can I?* (New York: Viking, 2022).

Day 23

Day 23
Bird Watching

My indoor office has a large window from which I can see a portion of my front yard as well as the street beyond. On the floor beside the window, I keep a soft rug for the dogs. While I'm in the office, they snuggle up on the rug with their chins resting upon the windowsill. They diligently watch for potential threats and quickly jump to their feet when they spot any person or animal. The volume and intensity of their barking alerts me to the nature of the "threat." Loud, frantic barks notify me that a human has ventured all the way onto my front porch. Intermittent barking reveals that a bird, squirrel, or other small animal is meandering through the yard. Sustained rhythmic barking lets me know that a dog and its owner have paused for a drink or treat at our front yard "dog-stop."

So, one beautiful morning, when the dogs jumped up and started whining, I wasn't sure what they were looking at. As they looked back and forth from me to the window with yips and grumbles, I knew they wanted me to take a look. I couldn't see anything from my chair at the desk, so I approached the window to investigate.

The scene was quite unusual and I immediately understood the dogs' distress. Right in the middle of our street, a vulture was snacking upon a snake. The scene was both disgusting and mesmerizing. The dogs and I stood transfixed as we watched the massive bird consume his tasty treat. Loving nature as I do, I was honored to observe the process without distracting the bird or scaring him away.

Day 23

The scenario reminds me of the way God watches over us. I believe that he loves to watch us when we are performing feats of faith, serving his people, and attaining personal victories. He is interested even when we are walking through mundane seasons of life and taking baby steps in our faith. He continues to watch over us even in moments when we are shameful, defeated, or downright disgusting.

Although we know that he continually watches over us, we often forget that he is near. Just as the vulture had no idea I was watching his every bite, we forget that God sees every intimate detail of our lives. According to Psalm 33:13–15, "From heaven the Lord looks down and sees all mankind; from his dwelling place he watches all who live on earth—he who forms the hearts of all, who considers everything they do."

We've already talked about how an awareness of God's presence should evoke both joy and caution. Today, I would like to point out that an awareness of his attention should foster greater authenticity and transparency in our relationship with him, more specifically in our prayer life. He is already aware of every gory detail and shameful situation. Fancy prayers full of sugar-coated confessions don't fool the Father. Let's, instead, pray over our hidden fears and confess our deepest sins. Let's allow our Father to shine light upon the darkest corners of our souls. In reality, he has already seen them. He is simply watching and waiting until we are ready to invite him in.

Father, thank you for watching over me with love and compassion. Help me live with a constant awareness of your presence. Grow my faith so that I'm not afraid of your nearness, but comforted by it. Teach me to pray without holding back my secret sins and deepest fears. Give me a longing for deeper intimacy with you that trumps every carnal desire and spiritual compromise. Empower me to be more faithful and transparent in my prayer life. Transform me increasingly into Christ's likeness as I continue to lean into your presence. In Jesus' name, Amen.

Personal Reflection

Meditate on the authenticity of your prayer life. Do you bring your deepest fears, darkest secrets, and hidden struggles to your Father? Do you refrain from praying over certain topics because you don't want to change, even though you know the situation(s) dishonor God? Simply tell your Father how you feel. Ask him to soften hardened places of your heart. Ask him to take away any desires that dishonor him. Ask him to empower and equip you to overcome your deepest fears. As you pray, practice listening for God's voice. (You may want to review the Personal Reflection from Day 21.) Finally, before you conclude, remember to pray through day 5 of your "handy prayer."

_____

_____

_____

_____

_____

_____

_____

_____

_____

Day 24
Dismals Canyon

Dismals Canyon is a fascinating and beautiful place. Known for its "glowworms," the canyon is the only place in the U.S. and one of the few sites in the world where the phosphorescent creatures can be found. Yet, even when the glowworms aren't in season, visiting the canyon is a memorable experience. It's also an experience that requires a certain level of physical conditioning.

Getting into the canyon requires a trek down a considerable number of stairs. Once you arrive, however, you feel as though you've traveled back in time to a prehistoric era. The sound of burbling waterfalls fills the air. Every surface is covered in thick, green moss because the massive trees and rock formations prevent direct sunlight from reaching the canyon floor. The twist and turns of the canyon, in conjunction with the lush vegetation, shrink the world to your immediate surroundings and add to the atmosphere of otherworldliness.

I've only hiked through the canyon a couple of times, but like the jasmine in City Park, the experience evokes the sensation of being surrounded. Unlike the jasmine in City Park, however, the surroundings at Dismals can begin to feel oppressive. And that was exactly how we felt on our first visit.

Not knowing the terrain well, we were grossly underprepared. We'd looked at the map, and learned that the trail itself isn't very long. Thus, we hadn't brought a substantial amount of water and we'd carried only a few snacks. There were however, several factors for which we had not accounted. First, the steps down to the trail were so lengthy that we were all dripping with sweat by the time we got to the trail. Second, the trail was not well marked and we couldn't see more than a few meters in front of us. So, we meandered off of the trail on numerous occasions, substantially lengthening our journey. Further, we could never identify the turn-around point of the hike, reversing our direction only when we began to see "private property" signs.

Needless to say, we quickly wilted in the Alabama heat, and our water ran out long before the hike ended. By the time we made our way back to the parking lot after a 3.5 hour hike, we were dehydrated and exhausted. Although the terrain was beautiful, I've never been so joyful to see my big red truck.

Like the hike at Dismals, our lives can sometimes seem oppressive. We feel surrounded and entrapped by responsibilities, worries, and trials. Perhaps we have work-related stress on one side, health concerns on another, relational conflict on another, and financial strain on yet another. Our concerns grow until they fill our field of vision, and we start to lose our way. Cut off from avenues of refreshing, we begin to feel exhausted, hopeless, and lost.

Yet, we are never lost and we are never alone. Our Father surrounds, protects, and provides for us. Even when we can't see past our worries, he can see the entire path ahead. David offers this reassurance: "Those who trust in the Lord are as secure as Mount Zion; they will not be defeated but will endure forever. Just as the mountains surround Jerusalem, so the Lord surrounds his people, both now and forever," (Psalm 125:1–2).

God wants us to know that he surrounds us with the security of his presence. Our trials don't have us surrounded because our Father is guarding us on all sides. If we trust him, he won't let anything sneak up, knock us down, or lead us astray.

Day 24

Although I was tired and thirsty when I was surrounded by the forest canyon, I wasn't afraid. I knew where I was because I have a strong sense of direction. Even when I couldn't see the trail ahead or find the trail at all, I wasn't worried, because I knew which direction to walk. Even if we don't know what is ahead of us, even when we aren't sure what to expect from next month, next week, or tomorrow, we can know where we are—safe in God's protection—and in which direction we should proceed—toward our Father.

If you start to feel surrounded, remember that you are . . . by God. He's got you on every side! You don't have to be able to see past your trials, you just have to keep moving toward your Father.

Heavenly Father, thank you for surrounding me with your presence. Thank you for granting me your protection and provision. Forgive me for allowing the concerns of life to consume my field of vision. Teach me to trust in your protective care and live with peace in my heart. Help me surrender my worries to you as I rest in your strong arms. I pray that I would be so immersed in your presence that others would experience your love through me. In Jesus' name, Amen.

Personal Reflection

On Day 7, you meditated on your mental and emotional response to God's constant presence. You asked God to point out any thoughts or behaviors that are dishonoring to his presence, and you prayed to dwell in his presence more fully. Revisit any notes you wrote down, then revise or reaffirm your impressions and objectives. Additionally, ask God to help you fix your gaze on his comforting presence instead of focusing on your concerns.

Growth, Gardens, & Grace

Day 25
Hiking Hazards

Yesterday I told you about my family's hike in Dismals Canyon, during which we got slightly lost and extremely worn-out. In addition to our depleted water supply, the steep inclines, rocky obstacles, and thick undergrowth made an already challenging hike excruciating. During moments of physical and mental strain like these, I always think of Isaiah 26:7–8. The prophet teaches, "But for those who are righteous, the way is not steep and rough. You are a God who does what is right, and you smooth out the path ahead of them. Lord, we show our trust in you by obeying your laws; our heart's desire is to glorify your name." When I'm dripping with sweat and gasping for breath, the idea of a smooth, level path is heavenly. When the rocky terrain clears, my relief is immediate—I can breathe easily, my muscles stop burning, and I can walk without straining, at least for the moment.

Although God doesn't smooth the terrain of my self-inflicted hiking adventures, he does smooth the pathway of our lives. He leads us in the right direction and re-directs us when we stray. He goes before us and behind us, preparing the way and guarding our back. His presence literally surrounds us, as we've discussed in several previous devotionals.

At the same time, we must partner with God to prepare ourselves for the journey. Just as I need food and water for long hikes, we must nourish ourselves by drinking of his living water and dining on the meat of his Word. Further, just as walking with my loved ones makes the hike more fun and the obstacles less daunting, doing life with our spiritual family gets us through the rockiest patches of life.

Let me also offer a concluding word of caution—if we wander a long way off of the trail, we'll have a long, hard hike back. As the verses above imply, we can stick to his smooth path by obeying his Word. So, let's gear up, grab our friends, get on the right path, and go for a great hike!

Lord, thank you for going before and behind me to prepare the way and protect my back. I trust that your ways are good and perfect. Give me the discipline to nourish my soul and spirit so that I'll be strong enough for any path upon which you place me. I repent of doubting you and pray that you would teach me to obey out of faith rather than fear. Give me the spiritual discernment to realize that even when the path seems steeper and rockier than I expect, you've already cleared the way and provided the resources I need to endure the journey. In Jesus' name, Amen.

Personal Reflection

Prayerfully meditate on the journey of your life. Are you equipping yourself to navigate difficult terrain? Are you walking in obedience so that you avoid any off-road obstacles? Are you walking with loved ones who will help you hike up the hills when you get tired? As you self-evaluate, ask God to show you at least one step you can take to stay on the path he has cleared for you, get back to his smooth path, and navigate rocky terrain with his help.

_____

_____

_____

_____

Day 25

Day 26
Well-Worn Paths

If you know me, you know that I'm a country girl. I was born and raised in Alabama. I even drive a red pickup truck. As a child, I lived in the country on a small farm. Our driveway was a long, gravel road that my sister and I would walk up and down all summer long. On other occasions, we would get in the truck and ride into the pastures and fields. The old dirt roads had been traveled so many times that the truck would almost drive itself in the big dirt tire ruts.

Recently, as I was riding my bike along an old country highway, I saw a path that reminded me of those roads from my childhood. It cut right through the middle of a field filled with crops. The pathway was so worn that no plants or grass grew across the two deep tire ruts.

I love those old roads because they remind me of an important truth from God's Word, similar to the smooth paths that we discussed yesterday. In Psalm 25:4–5, David prays, "Show me the right path, O Lord; point out the road for me to follow. Lead me by your truth and teach me, for you are the God who saves me. All day long I put my hope in you."

We all have well-worn paths in our lives. Some may be good, and some may be not-so-good. Either way, the more we travel down these well-worn pathways, the more automatic they become. When we go down the same pathway time and again, just like truck tires on an old country road, we wear the treads a little deeper. Then, if we ever decide to take a different path or change direction, we encounter extreme difficulty getting out of those old ruts.

Fortunately, Jesus empowers us to forge a new path, and he shows us the way to go. Although he doesn't provide a literal map, he does provide signposts in Scripture. Like street signs and stop lights, God's Word directs us toward the safe, healthy, and smooth path our Father has laid before us.

If we are stuck on an old path, it might take some time and effort to get our wheels out of the ruts. Eventually though, if we stick with our new habits, they'll become just as well-worn and easily traveled as the old ones.

In the meantime, we may need some metaphorical or literal signage to keep us out of the ruts. For over 15 years, I've kept a decorative sign with Psalm 25:4–5 on my kitchen counter. The wise words are a constant reminder to my willful heart that God's path is better than my own.

Heavenly Father, Thank you for showing me the paths that lead to life. Reveal areas of my life that dishonor you, cause harm to others, or keep me from the good and perfect pathway you've laid before me. Forgive me for going my own way instead of following you. Teach me to heed the clear signs you've provided in Scripture. Empower me to break out of old ruts and create pathways that bring joy and peace into my life and the lives of those around me. In Jesus' Name, Amen.

Personal Reflection

Prayerfully consider your well-worn paths. Are you stuck in any old ruts or harmful habits that are keeping you from health and growth? Ask God to show you at least one pathway that he wants to help you redirect. Then get creative and make a few signposts to help you keep moving in the right direction. They don't have to be literal signs, just anything that reminds you to stay on the right path.

Day 27
Ugly Caterpillars and Beautiful Butterflies
— Part 1

Among my most interesting plants is my passion vine. When I first purchased the plant, I potted it in a coconut liner basket and set it on the ground by the fence. It quickly climbed to the top of the fence, grew large alien looking flowers, and produced several passion fruits. The large, messy vine was too unwieldy to move over the winter, so I let it die off, hoping it would return in the spring.

And return, it did! The passion plant had grown right through the coconut liner and rooted itself in the ground. Under the surface of the soil, the vine had birthed a brood of offshoots as well! Passion vines began growing everywhere within a 10 foot radius of the original.

I now know that passion vine is invasive. (You should not plant passion vine in your yard!) Nonetheless, I pulled up the shoots I didn't want and allowed the rest to continue climbing the fence once again. Watching the plant flourish, I eagerly anticipated the soon-to-come flowers and fruits.

Sadly, no flowers would be blooming on my passion plant. One morning as I strolled the perimeter of my yard checking on various plants, I saw that a ravenous horde of caterpillars had decimated my lush vine.

I was horrified. The caterpillars weren't cute and fuzzy like the ones that had delighted me as a child. They were slimy looking burnt umber creatures with black spikes all over their bodies. Many were large enough that I could see their fat mouths chomping on the leaves and stems of the vine.

Initially mistaking the creatures for a similar caterpillar with poisonous spikes, I nearly sprayed them with pesticide. Before doing so, however, I made a quick social media post, hoping to find a better solution.

Almost immediately, a fellow nature lover corrected my mistaken identification. She explained that the creatures were actually gulf fritillary caterpillars, a species that dines exclusively on passion vine. The best part is that after eating their fill of passion vine, they pupate and transform into beautiful auburn-hued butterflies. Once again I was horrified, but this time I was horrified that I'd almost killed the lovely little creatures.

Like all caterpillars, my gulf fritillaries illustrate a principle we encounter often in Scripture. Paul explains, "If anyone is in Christ, *they have become* a new creature. The old has gone. Look! The new has arrived! And all these *new things* are from God!" (2 Corinthians 5:17, my translation). When we accept Jesus, he transforms us into a new creation, a metamorphosis that takes place in an instant, yet also continues for a lifetime.

Perhaps you are feeling like an ugly caterpillar. Let me remind you that if you've accepted Jesus as your Savior, he has transformed you into a beautiful new creation. Your new life isn't accompanied by a list of exceptions like the small print at the bottom of a legal contract. No matter what you've done, where you've been, or how ugly your past, Jesus is transforming you into a masterpiece!

Jesus, thank you for the free gift of salvation and transformation. Thank you for wiping away my ugly sin with your unconditional grace. Teach me to lean into your lordship rather than reverting to the distasteful patterns of my past. Give me a desire to walk in the fullness of my new life, and

Day 27

empower me to walk worthy of my calling. Help me reflect your love to such an extent that other people are drawn to your beauty. In your name, Amen.

Personal Reflection

Our brains operate in such a way that we tend to actualize the descriptors placed upon us, even if subconsciously. For example, if I think I'm a slow runner, I won't try as hard to run fast. If people tell me I'm dumb (and if I agree), I won't try as hard to learn. Conversely, if I think I'm a kind person, I'll make more of an effort to be kind. If people tell me I'm good at sports (and if I agree), I'll be more likely to hone my athletic abilities. So today, reflect on your own self-perception. Ask God to help you align your self-assessment with his declaration that you are a new creation.

Day 28
Ugly Caterpillars and Beautiful Butterflies
— Part 2

Yesterday I told you about the gulf fritillaries that took over my passion vine. My initial distaste was quickly replaced by joy as the ugly caterpillars transformed into beautiful butterflies. Their transformation reminds me that even in my ugliest moments, I am a beautiful new creation through Christ. The process also reminds me that God has likewise transformed all of his children, even the ones I find unappealing.

Along such lines, our Father doesn't judge or appraise people the way that you and I do, and when we accept Jesus as Lord, he calls us to align our process of evaluation with his. Moreover, he calls us to act upon our new perspective. In the same passage of Scripture, we discussed yesterday, Paul teaches,

> *Because we understand our fearful responsibility to the Lord, we work hard to persuade others. . . . If it seems we are crazy, it is to bring glory to God. And if we are in our right minds, it is for your benefit. Either way, Christ's love controls us. Since we believe that Christ died for all, we also believe that we have all died to our old life. He died for everyone so that those who receive his new life will no longer live for themselves. Instead, they will live for Christ, who died and*

Day 28

> *was raised for them. So we have stopped evaluating others from a human point of view.*
>
> *2 Corinthians 5:11, 13–16a*

The world may look at a person and see a slimy worm, but we are called to look beyond the surface. Through Christ, we see their potential to become something beautiful, even if the process of transformation hasn't begun yet.

Allow me to illustrate once again with my gulf fritillaries, two of whom came to live inside my house. Because Abel sees the wonder in everything, he adopted two of the fat caterpillars as pets. He re-homed them from the vines in the yard to mason jars on our kitchen table. He faithfully cleaned the jars of droppings and hydrated the caterpillars with droplets of water. He daily searched the yard for passion vine leaves and kept his pets well nourished.

As our supply of passion vine quickly dwindled, he worried that we would run out of food before the caterpillars pupated. Just in time, however, both attached themselves to the top of the jar and began to weave cocoons. A few weeks later, the dry, brown husks cracked open to reveal two stunningly beautiful butterflies. With great joy, we returned them to our yard to continue the cycle of creating more butterflies.

Just as Abel cared for his unappealing little pets, God calls us to foster the flourishing of his sons and daughters. Let's learn to love all people—not just the ones who are already lovely—and nourish them from the overflow of our own hearts.

Father, thank you for giving me new life and transforming the way I think. Teach me to see the potential in all people, even those the world regards as distasteful. Empower me to love the unlovely and extend your grace to each person who crosses my path. Give me creative ideas and abundant resources to create spaces for people to encounter your love. Open my eyes to opportunities to foster flourishing and facilitate transformation. In Jesus' name, Amen.

Personal Reflection

Yesterday, you worked on your self-perception. Today, practice evaluating others through the lens of your new life in Christ. How can you facilitate the flourishing of others and love the unlovely?

_____

_____

_____

_____

_____

_____

_____

_____

_____

_____

_____

_____

_____

Day 29
The Very Hungry Caterpillar

I'm obsessed with luna moths. One of the largest moth species in North America, the elegant green creatures boast a wingspan of up to four inches. The common name "luna moth" is appropriate both because the creatures are nocturnal, but also because of the crescent shaped markings on their wings. Although they're active primarily in spring and summer, which is typical for moths, they can be found year-round in warmer states like Louisiana and Florida.

Growing up in the country, the beautiful moths were a daily sight for me. Each morning, I would wake up and gaze at the vibrant, minty wings covering my window screens. Even as a child, I knew I was seeing something special. As an adult now living in a suburban neighborhood, I rarely see luna moths anymore. Due to their short life span and nocturnal disposition, most humans rarely encounter the enchanting creatures.

Luna moths begin life as a saturniidae caterpillar, or giant silkworm. Since the moths don't eat, have digestive systems, or even have mouths, they must eat as much as possible during the caterpillar phase. In fact, luna moth larvae spend 2 to 4 times the average span as very hungry caterpillars. Then, once they pupate and emerge from the cocoon, they live only a brief 7–10 days.

Soon after emergence, the female moth will emit a pheromone and attract a male to fertilize her eggs. She then spends the remainder of her life depositing eggs upon specific plants that her progeny will consume. In short, the entire purpose of the adult luna moth is to reproduce before it dies.

We are similarly called to reproduce ourselves as followers of Christ. Although each of us has a specific purpose, the guiding principle of our entire lives should be to create new life through spreading the Gospel.

Just before ascending to heaven, Jesus exhorted his disciples to reproduce themselves.

> *Jesus came and told his disciples, "I have been given all authority in heaven and on earth. Therefore, go and make disciples of all the nations, baptizing them in the name of the Father and the Son and the Holy Spirit. Teach these new disciples to obey all the commands I have given you. And be sure of this: I am with you always, even to the end of the age."*
>
> ### *Matthew 28:18–20*

Jesus' call for more disciples doesn't stem from a superficial desire for more fame or followers. Rather, our Savior wants all of his people to experience the new life he offers. Equally important, our Father wants all of his children to be reconciled with him so they can spend eternity in his presence. I get excited just thinking about it, and I want to be sure all the people I love are there as well!

Because we are each called and created for a unique purpose, the means by which we grow God's kingdom will take different forms. However, we are ALL called to spread the Gospel through our words and actions. Even if we aren't a pastor, preacher, or teacher, Jesus has equipped us to reproduce your light and life in this world!

Jesus, thank you for allowing me to spread the Gospel and offer new life to others. Give me the courage to speak boldly about my faith and the

Day 29

integrity to live it out. Help me remember that my primary purpose in this world is to raise up disciples and lead people to your love. Equip me with the resources I need to be successful and open my eyes to the opportunities around me. In Jesus' name, Amen.

Personal Reflection

Be mindful of your primary purpose today. Look for opportunities to share the Gospel through your words and actions!

Day 30
The Last Summer

By now, you should be well into the season of spring and in proximity to Resurrection Sunday, i.e., Easter. We've already been discussing the new life Jesus makes available through his death, burial, and resurrection. In that light, let's shift our hearts toward a more reverent posture and examine some of the details just prior to his crucifixion. We'll begin with the Last Supper and the sacrament of communion that Jesus instituted during the meal. As we revisit familiar verses, try to imagine yourself at the table with Jesus and view the events with fresh eyes.

On the night before Jesus was crucified, he celebrated Passover with his disciples. As he ate with his closest friends, Jesus conducted the first communion service. Matthew records that Jesus took some bread and blessed it, then broke it in pieces and gave it to the disciples, saying, "Take this and eat it, for this is my body," (Matthew 26:26).

Jesus knew that after the meal he would endure unimaginable suffering, and the bread represented his soon to be broken body. Our Lord would be mocked, tormented, beaten, and nailed to a cross. Even at that very moment, Jesus was being betrayed by one of his closest friends, Judas. Yet, he willingly endured each agony so that we could receive healing in mind, body and spirit.

After breaking the bread, Jesus took a cup of wine and blessed it. "He gave it to [the disciples] and said, 'Each of you drink from it, for this is my blood, which confirms the covenant between God and his people. It is poured out as a sacrifice to forgive the sins of many,'" (Matthew 26:27b–28). The wine represented the blood of Christ that would be shed so that each human could enter into a covenant relationship with God.

Prior to Jesus' sacrifice, our sins prevented us from approaching the presence of our Father. Yet, the blood of Christ covers and cleanses every blemish so that we are made worthy to have a personal relationship with the Lord both now and for all eternity. By reminding us of Jesus' sacrifice, communion reminds us of just how deeply our Savior cares for us.

The sacrament doesn't magically make us holier, but rather, helps us grow more firmly rooted in our relationship with Jesus. Paul exhorts, "You should examine yourself before eating the bread and drinking the cup," (1 Corinthians 11:28). In other words, as we partake, we meditate on God's love, Christ's sacrifice, and our own sin. As we commune with our Lord, we remember just how much we need a Savior, we express gratitude for his continuing work in our lives, and we repent of any thoughts, words, or deeds that dishonor him. So, as we conclude for today, let's ask the Spirit to examine our hearts and bring us into closer communion with Jesus.

Lord, thank you for enduring unimaginable suffering so that I could receive hope and healing. Thank you for giving me new life and opportunities to flourish. I ask you to reveal any areas in my life that aren't submitted to you. Expose any patterns of thought or behaviors that don't honor you. Forgive me where I've failed you and sinned against you. Please replace any areas of sin or bondage with the freedom that comes from your work at the cross. In Jesus' name, Amen.

Personal Reflection

Although communion is often a corporate act, the sacrament can also be practiced in solitude. So, let's prepare to partake right now. Take a moment, first, to gather your elements. You can use wine, juice, or virtually any beverage, as well as bread, crackers, or any small morsel of food. The items you use are far less important than the meaning behind them. Second, take a moment to allow the Spirit to examine your heart. Practice the discipline of listening that we discussed on days 21 and 23. Confess any sin that God reveals and express gratitude for his sacrifice. Third, re-read the second, third, and fourth paragraphs above to guide you through receiving the elements.

Day 31
Communion Conundrum

Yesterday we talked about the Last Supper and the sacrament of communion. Knowing we would need such moments of reflection, our Savior instituted the practice before his earthly life ended. Whether we partake alone or in a group setting, the practice helps us enter into a moment of intimacy with Jesus. In a world of constant stimuli, the ritual draws our focus off of our distractions and onto our Savior.

In addition to those moments of private meditation in the presence of Jesus, communion is a powerful corporate act. As we read yesterday, when Jesus instituted the sacrament, his disciples partook *together*. Thus, while communion is a time of personal intimacy with Jesus, the practice is also a statement of our unity as God's people. When we partake together, we affirm that we are all part of Christ's body. We confirm our relationship as brothers and sisters in the family of God. We declare our continuing allegiance to one another and to our Heavenly Father.

Just as communion is a reminder of Christ's work on our behalf, the rite is also a reminder that we are one family on one mission together. Paul explains, "When we bless the cup at the Lord's Table, aren't we sharing in the blood of Christ? And when we break the bread, aren't we sharing in the body of Christ? And though we are many, we all eat from one loaf of bread, showing that we are one body," (1 Corinthians 10:16–17).

Only a few verses later, as Paul continues his letter to the Corinthian church, he chastises them for forgetting the significance of communion. Strife, division, and selfishness characterized their gatherings. The Lord's Supper had become no more than a meal, and even worse, a meal from which needy members of the congregation were being excluded. Paul laments,

> *But in the following instructions, I cannot praise you. For it sounds as if more harm than good is done when you meet together. First, I hear that there are divisions among you when you meet as a church, and to some extent I believe it. . . . When you meet together, you are not really interested in the Lord's Supper. For some of you hurry to eat your own meal without sharing with others. As a result, some go hungry while others get drunk. What? Don't you have your own homes for eating and drinking? Or do you really want to disgrace God's church and shame the poor? What am I supposed to say? Do you want me to praise you? Well, I certainly will not praise you for this!*
>
> **1 Corinthians 11:17–18, 20–22**

While we probably haven't mishandled communion in the same way as the Corinthians, the likelihood is high that we've disregarded the unity of our faith family or the larger Church at some point. In addition to the internal harm that strife and selfishness cause, divisions in the church harm our witness to those who don't know Christ. Why would anyone want to become part of a group of people who don't even like each other? So, as we meditate on the significance of communion, let's remember to love those with whom we commune most closely.

Day 31

Jesus, thank you for sacrificing yourself so that I can enjoy a personal relationship with my Heavenly Father. I praise you for your perfect holiness, goodness, and love. Help me to live in a way that reflects your love and honors your sacrifice. I repent of fostering disunity and division among your children. Show me how I can, instead, foster love and grace among those closest to me. Help me to see your people through your eyes and selflessly serve my brothers and sisters in Christ. In Jesus' name, Amen.

Personal Reflection

Prayerfully ask God to show you a few practical ways you can foster unity within your faith family or in the larger body of Christ.

Day 32
Meaningful Mementos

The last couple of days, we've been discussing the institution of communion. As a pastor, I've led communion more times than I can count. I've also performed countless baptisms. Therefore, during one recent communion service, I began to ponder why each of us is only commanded to be baptized once, yet Jesus calls us to celebrate communion repeatedly.

Allow me to share what I learned from my meditation, prayer, and study. Paul writes,

> *On the night when he was betrayed, the Lord Jesus took some bread and gave thanks to God for it. Then he broke it in pieces and said, "This is my body, which is given for you. Do this in remembrance of me." In the same way, [Jesus] took the cup of wine after supper, saying, "This cup is the new covenant between God and his people—an agreement confirmed with my blood. Do this in remembrance of me as often as you drink it." For every time you eat this bread and drink this cup, you are announcing the Lord's death until he comes again.*
>
> ***1 Corinthians 11:23b–26***

In other words, Jesus tells us to partake of communion in *remembrance* of him.

Day 32

As he often does, the Lord helped me understand this principle through the lens of my garden. In my garden alone, I'm surrounded by a wide range of mementos that remind me of joyful moments. A cute stone gnome I purchased while visiting family in Kentucky sits by my front patio, and an ancient Canaanite ballista excavated while working in Israel sits by my back patio. Throughout the garden, I also have a star hibiscus transplanted from my Gram's house 20 years ago, a large agave I dug up and brought home from a family trip to Florida, and a stained-glass stepping stone my Mom made when Asher was born.

In short, when we want to keep meaningful memories fresh, we keep mementos nearby. Similarly, God instructs us to create reminders of his work in our lives. Although we scoff at the Israelites, who whined and disobeyed even after witnessing numerous miracles, the truth is that you and I are just as fickle. Thus, the Lord encourages us to place reminders in our lives to help us stand strong in our faith.

In the Old Testament, God commanded the Israelites to wear his commands upon their wrists and foreheads so that his words would be foremost in their actions and thoughts (Deuteronomy 6:8). Later on, when the people crossed the Jordan into the Promised Land, the Lord commanded them to create a pile of stones as a memorial (Joshua 4:4–7).

Communion serves a similar purpose for you and I. When I partake of communion, I'm reminded to obey the statutes of my Lord, not out of obligation, but out of gratitude. The bread and wine, like the stones in the Jordan River, are a memorial of crossing from my old life to a new one.

As for the distinction between communion and baptism, communion is a deeply personal moment with our Savior, while baptism is a public celebration. Baptism is an outward declaration of our inward transformation. It is a public statement that we've decided to become part of God's family and live according to Kingdom values. Although there is nothing wrong with being baptized a second time to recommit our life or reaffirm our faith, we aren't commanded to do so. Yet, we are called to take communion on a regular basis because Jesus knows we need regular reminders of his sacrificial love.

Jesus, thank you for allowing your body to be broken and your blood to be spilled as a ransom for my sins. Help me to grasp the gravity of your sacrifice and live accordingly. Teach me to walk with an awareness of your sacrifice on my behalf and live in fullness of gratitude. Although I can never repay the price you paid, I pray that my life would bring you glory and build your Kingdom. In your name, Amen.

Personal Reflection

If you attend a church that regularly partakes of communion, consider how you can place additional reminders in your life of Jesus' work on your behalf. If you don't attend church or if your faith family doesn't regularly partake, consider adding a weekly time of personal communion to your calendar.

Day 32

Day 33
Gardener of Eden

As we continue to meditate upon the death and resurrection of our Savior, I would like to shine light on a few details that are often overlooked. The Gospel authors explain how Jesus makes atonement for our sins and gives us new life, yet they also subtly reveal how Jesus' actions fulfill God's plan to restore all of creation. In particular, I want to show you how John portrays Jesus as a new Adam—a new gardener of Eden!

In his Gospel, John informs us that Jesus and his disciples walked to the Garden of Gethsemane after sharing their Passover meal (John 18:1). While there, Jesus was betrayed, bound, and forced from the garden. I can't help but see an echo of Genesis 3, in which Adam and Eve, betrayed and deceived by the Serpent, were exiled from the Garden of Eden as a result of their sin. Although Jesus was sinless, he willingly bore the consequences we all deserve.

As John continues, he reveals that Jesus was buried in yet another garden: "The place of crucifixion was near a garden, where there was a new tomb, never used before. And so, because it was the day of preparation for the Jewish Passover and since the tomb was close at hand, they laid Jesus there," (John 19:41-42). Three days later, Mary stood and wept by Jesus' tomb. John recounts, "She turned to leave and saw someone standing there. It was Jesus, but she didn't recognize him. 'Dear woman, why are you crying?' Jesus asked her. 'Who are you looking for?' [But] she thought he was the gardener," (John 20:14–15a).

Day 33

Mary's mistaken identification has often been attributed to the fact that she met Jesus in a garden. Indeed, encountering a gardener in a garden wouldn't be unusual. However, I think John conveys a deeper truth. Gardens are significant from the opening lines of Genesis to the closing verses of Revelation, representing the space in which sinless humans dwell in the perfect presence of God. Thus, I believe the identification of Jesus as a gardener must be attributed to more than the blurry eyes of a weeping woman.

Although Adam and Eve were expelled from their garden, and Jesus was buried in one, our Savior rose again and emerged into a garden, restored and reunited with the Father. Jesus became the gardener that Adam and Eve had failed to be, planting seeds of the new creation. We'll talk more on the topic tomorrow, but for now, let's pray.

Jesus, thank you for enduring the humiliation, betrayal, and death that I deserve for my sins. Thank you for giving me new life and beginning the process of restoration for all creation. Help me reflect your image as a gardener as I seek to bring life to my world. Show me how I can be an agent of healing among my fellow humans and in the natural world. In your name, Amen.

Personal Reflection

Prayerfully meditate and write down a few ways you can bring healing, restoration, and life through your words and actions. Be intentional to begin implementing your ideas today.

_____

_____

_____

Day 34
Birth Pains

Yesterday we discussed Jesus' role as a gardener—a new Adam who restores our relationship with God and plants the seeds of a new Eden. With his resurrection, Jesus inaugurates the new creation and becomes the first fruits of a new era (1 Corinthians 15:21–23). Today, we'll shift from the words of John to the Gospel of Matthew to explore the crucifixion and resurrection in more detail.

Matthew records a series of supernatural phenomena that took place when Jesus died:

> *Then Jesus shouted out again, and he released his spirit. At that moment the curtain in the sanctuary of the Temple was torn in two, from top to bottom. The earth shook, rocks split apart, and tombs opened. The bodies of many godly men and women who had died were raised from the dead. They left the cemetery after Jesus' resurrection, went into the holy city of Jerusalem, and appeared to many people.*
>
> **Matthew 27:51–53**

The release of God's Spirit from Jesus' body was so powerful that the ground shook, the earth burst open, and dead people returned to life. Forgive me for the comparison, but I can't help but picture an ancient Ghostbusters movie. Instead of ghosts strolling through modern-day New York City, previously dead people began walking the streets of ancient Jerusalem!

Related passages of Scripture help us understand the events to an even greater degree. More than 500 years before Christ, Ezekiel prophesied,

> *Thus says the Lord God, "Behold, I, myself, will split open your graves, and I will cause you to rise up from your tombs, my people; and I will bring you to the land of Israel. Then you will know that I am the Lord, when I open your graves and raise you from your tombs, my people. Then I will put my Spirit in you, and you will come to life!"*
>
> **Ezekiel 37:12–14a (my translation)**

The rising of the dead from their graves was an established and expected sign that God's redemption was at hand and his Spirit was bringing new life to his people.

The ripping of the temple veil and shaking of the ground are also clear indications that God's Spirit was moving. No longer would God's presence be inaccessible to humanity, hidden behind a curtain. As Jesus released his Spirit, God's presence began to fill all of creation. His movement was so powerful that the earth literally trembled.

Paul compares such upheavals to the process of birth. He explains,

> *Against its will, all creation was subjected to God's curse. But with eager hope, the creation looks forward to the day when it will join God's children in glorious freedom from death and decay. For we know that all creation has been groaning as in the pains of childbirth right up to the present time.*
>
> **Romans 8:20–22**

Day 34

Like a woman experiencing labor prior to bearing new life, the natural world experiences labor pains as we approach the birth of the new creation.

Jesus' death and resurrection were the beginning of the end. At the cross, he inaugurated the final phase of God's redemptive plan. The supernatural signs were a foreshadowing in miniature of events that will happen later on a cosmic scale. Just as the godly men and women from Jerusalem rose from their graves, everyone who has placed their faith in Christ will rise from the dead when he returns. Just as the earth shook and the rocks split apart, the entirety of creation will be shaken as it is transformed and restored to perfection. Although the day will be fearful for those who don't know God, Paul reminds us to look forward to Jesus' return "with eager hope" and joyfully anticipate the glorious freedom all of creation will experience.

Lord, thank you for willingly going to the cross to begin the final phase of redemption for all of creation. Help me walk in the fullness of my new life as I resist old habits that invite death and destruction in my life. Teach me how to live in the light of your redemptive work—with hope, joy, and expectation. Fill me with such eager hope for your return that I can't resist telling others about the new life you offer. Give me a constant awareness that the way I live now impacts my own eternity and the eternity of those I love. In Jesus' name, Amen.

Personal Reflection

How can you bring a greater awareness of eternity into your daily routine? Read through your notes from yesterday and continue implementing strategies for bringing healing and restoration to the world. As you do so, consider the eternal impact of your words and actions.

Growth, Gardens, & Grace

Day 35
Inspiration — Part 1

Over the last few days, we've been discussing the creation-wide impact of Jesus' death and resurrection. Our Savior died to take the consequences of our sins, and he rose from the dead to give us new life. His death and resurrection also reversed the process of death and decay that the sin of Adam and Eve introduced into creation. Today I would like to show you another Scriptural connection between the pure state of Eden prior to sin and Jesus' power to restore creation to that perfect state.

Yesterday, we read a portion of Ezekiel's "dry bones" prophecy. Although he spoke to the nation of Judah, his words ring true for all of God's people. As Ezekiel described the future redemption and restoration God would bring about, the prophet relayed God's promise to *breathe life into* his people. Ezekiel reported, "This is what the Sovereign Lord says: 'Look! I am going to put breath into you and make you live again! I will put flesh and muscles on you and cover you with skin. I will put breath into you, and you will come to life,'" (Ezekiel 37:5–6a).

The connection between God's breath and human life originates in the opening chapters of Scripture when God breathes into Adam (Genesis 2:7). As God breathes into humanity, he doesn't simply impart biological life, but spiritual existence. Thus, when the Father promised to breathe into Judah and make them live again, he offered physical restoration *and* spiritual redemption.

Growth, Gardens, & Grace

This knowledge, then, equips us to understand Jesus' interaction with his disciples following his own resurrection.

> *That Sunday evening the disciples were meeting behind locked doors because they were afraid of the Jewish leaders. Suddenly, Jesus was standing there among them! "Peace be with you," he said. As he spoke, he showed them the wounds in his hands and his side. They were filled with joy when they saw the Lord! Again he said, "Peace be with you. As the Father has sent me, so I am sending you." Then he breathed on them and said, "Receive the Holy Spirit."*
>
> **John 20:19–22**

In this passage, I see Jesus giving new spiritual life to his disciples and resurrecting their hope.

Certainly, the disciples' faith was in dire straits. Notice that in John 20:19, they were hiding behind locked doors in fear, and from Mark 14:50, we learn that they had fled in terror when Jesus was arrested. From Mark 26, we learn that Peter had denied the Savior three times and "wept bitterly" over his spiritual failure (Mark 26:65). Yet, when Jesus returned, he didn't chastise the disciples for failing to understand his teaching or criticize their lack of faith. The Lord simply breathed into their despondent hearts, washing away their fear and restoring their faith. In doing so, he resurrected their ministry and reinvigorated their passion to spread God's love. The scene is so beautiful that I don't want to rush past it. Let's therefore pause here to reflect on the life-giving love of our Savior.

Jesus, thank you for breathing new life into me. Thank you for giving health to my body and my spirit. Forgive me for the times I've hidden my faith out of fear or failed to speak up on behalf of your goodness.

Day 35

Thank you for refusing to hold my sins against me and for accepting me just as I am. Just as you transformed the fear and sorrow of the disciples into peace and joy, I ask you to resurrect the lifeless parts of my heart. I ask you to reinvigorate my desire to share your love and spread the Gospel. In your name, Amen.

Personal Reflection

Take a few moments to think about the emotional rollercoaster the disciples experienced. I can't imagine how dejected they must have felt when Jesus was arrested and crucified; how betrayed that their Messiah had failed them; how terrified that they would follow in his crucified footsteps; how ashamed of their own failure to stand firm. In the span of 24 hours, the entire framework of their faith and the very purpose of their lives crumbled around them. Then, he reappeared—their living breathing Savior! With only a few words and one breath, Jesus gave new life and purpose to those who felt dead inside. As you meditate on the restoration of the disciples, think about any times in your own life during which you doubted your faith. Thank God for restoring your purpose, peace and joy. If you are currently in a devastating season of life, pour out your heart to God and allow the experience of the disciples to remind you that your own restoration is right around the corner.

_____

_____

_____

_____

_____

Day 36
Inspiration — Part 2

Yesterday we talked about the breath of God—a gift that both animates our physical bodies and our spiritual lives. The Father bestowed it upon humanity at creation, and Jesus bestows it upon his followers in preparation for the new creation. Today we'll continue talking about breath and its significance in our lives

As biological entities, breathing is essential for life. The process of respiration is so vital that our bodies manage it automatically. Receptors in our heart and blood vessels send signals to our brain with information about how much oxygen we need. For example, when we exercise, our receptors notify the brain that we need more oxygen, and the respiratory center of the brain accommodates by increasing the respiration rate. When physical exertion ceases, receptors let the brain know that the oxygen demand has decreased and respiration returns to normal.

Respiration is unique, however, among other automatic bodily functions. Unlike processes such as digestion and blood circulation, breathing can be controlled automatically *and* voluntarily. Athletes and musicians learn to breathe in such a way as to maximize performance. You and I can learn to breathe deeply in order to calm ourselves in stressful situations.

I believe that these two aspects of respiration—voluntary and automatic—serve as a helpful analogy for our spiritual lives. As physical creatures, we don't have to make any effort to stay alive. Our hearts, lungs, kidneys, brains, and other organs function without conscious control. Our spiritual life operates much the same way. Once we accept the free gift of new life from Christ, we are redeemed through no effort on our part. However, if we want to maintain a healthy body or a healthy spiritual life, we must take proactive steps. Just as deep breathing calms the nervous system, reduces stress hormones, and promotes healthy blood pressure, "breathing" God's spirit through prayer and Bible study brings life to our spirit.

In fact, both physical and spiritual respiration are described by the same word: inspiration. In biological terms, inspiration describes the intake of air. Spiritually speaking, inspiration refers to divine influence—the process of being filled with God's spirit such that we are stimulated to think, do, or say something. Over time, the term has shifted toward the more broad nuance of "motivation" or "infusion of imagination," but its origin has always been theologically rooted.[4]

Both spiritual and physical inspiration require focus, intention, and action. The behavioral control of breathing requires a mental decision which is then followed by a specific action—the intake of air. Similarly, being filled with a greater degree God's Spirit requires a mental decision followed by action. Growing more spiritually alive will never happen by accident. If we want to be inspired, we must seek inspiration! Job drew upon the inspiration of God to speak words of truth and righteousness (Job 27:1–6). The prophets "sought and inquired carefully" about salvation, and were inspired to share the Gospel message (1 Peter 1:10; 2 Peter 1:16–21). The words of Scripture are inspired by God, and searching them empowers us to draw nearer to Christ and be equipped for his service (1 Timothy 3:16–17; John 5:39).

---

[4] "The Inspirational History of *Inspiration*," Merriam-Webster, https://www.merriam-webster.com/dictionary/inspiration#note-1.

Day 36

Gathering together, just as the disciples did before and after Jesus' crucifixion, also invites the breath of God to inspire us. Despite the disciples' fearful state, Jesus appeared to them behind locked doors and breathed on them (John 20:19–22). When the disciples gathered for Pentecost, God's breath blew as a mighty wind and filled them with power (Acts 2:1–4). In Matthew 18:20, although he doesn't specifically mention breath, Jesus teaches that when two or more gather in his name, his presence is among us.

So, as we close, let's take a deep breath and set an intention to be inspired today!

Jesus, thank you for breathing life into my imperfect soul. Help me be intentional about seeking the inspiration you provide. Empower me to turn from every pattern of behavior or speech that breeds death and destruction. Give me a greater desire for your Spirit and your inspiration. Guide me toward habits that will foster my faith and deepen my understanding of your love. Reinvigorate the parts of my heart that are weary and give me fresh motivation to serve you with joy. In your name, Amen.

Personal Reflection

Today's reflection is two-fold.

- First, prayerfully meditate on how you can be more inspired in your spiritual life. Write down a few ideas below then choose one to try today.
- Second, recall that gathering with fellow believers is a powerful avenue for experiencing God's inspiration. Since we've recently discussed communion, consider inviting a family member, friend, or Bible study group to join you in partaking of communion and thanking Jesus for the new life he has given you.

Day 37
Wedding Feast

Recently Wesley and I celebrated our 22nd anniversary, so memories of our wedding are fresh in my mind. We began preparing for the wedding roughly 9 months in advance—choosing a dress, ordering flowers, selecting a caterer, and booking a venue. We met with our pastor for pre-marital counseling and read books on relational health. The night before the wedding, we rehearsed the service and enjoyed a rehearsal dinner with our families. Finally, on the day of the wedding, I spent all day getting hair, nails, and makeup done with my bridesmaids.

    I wanted everything to be perfect, as most brides do. Even now, when we celebrate anniversaries and special events, I prepare ahead of time. We block out the day on our calendars and make a restaurant reservation. On the day of our "date," I'll spend more time than usual doing my makeup and hair. I'll try on half of my closet searching for the perfect outfit. I'll even brainstorm a few things to talk about to make sure we have good dinner conversation.

    Now, of course, Wesley's love doesn't depend on me looking good or being a good conversationalist, but I prepare because I want to honor him and let him know that our time together is important to me. Can you imagine if, on our date night, I walked straight in from working in the garden? With sticks and leaves in my hair, sweaty clothes, and dirt under my fingernails, Wesley would politely decline to take me anywhere! I wouldn't be able to blame him because my disheveled state would convey that I don't place much value on our relationship.

So, on our anniversary, I began to meditate on the manner in which I approach time with my Lord. Since the Church is the bride of Christ, both collectively and individually, I should be intentional about preparing for my time with Jesus. As I evaluated some of my habits, I realized they were less than honoring toward my Lord. If I'm being honest, I have to admit that some days my prayer time takes place while I'm driving around town. Sometimes I get distracted during my quiet time and end up scrolling through social media or watering flowers. Sometimes I fail to get out of bed in time to spend time with my Savior. Thankfully, Jesus doesn't get angry when I neglect our relationship, but I know that when I am intentional about preparing my heart and eliminating distractions, I enjoy greater intimacy with him.

As we've discussed in detail over the last couple of weeks, we are now in the period prior to Jesus' final return. Our current phase of history is a bit like the preparation phase that takes place prior to a wedding. Just as I spent 9 months preparing for my wedding day, I should be diligent to prepare for Jesus' return. On that day, the celebration will be more glorious than any wedding in history. In Revelation, John describes his visions of that day.

> *Then I heard again what sounded like the shout of a vast crowd or the roar of mighty ocean waves or the crash of loud thunder:*
>
> *"Praise the Lord!*
> *For the Lord our God, the Almighty, reigns.*
> *Let us be glad and rejoice,*
> *and let us give honor to him.*
> *For the time has come for the wedding feast of the Lamb,*

Day 37

> *and his bride has prepared herself.*
> *She has been given the finest of pure white linen to wear."*
> *For the fine linen represents the good deeds of God's holy people.*
> *And the angel said to me, "Write this: Blessed are those who are invited to the wedding feast of the Lamb." And he added, "These are true words that come from God."*
>
> **Revelation 19:6–9**

How are your wedding preparations coming along? Are you spotless and clean or do you have leaves in your hair and dirt on your shoes? Let's plan and prepare like our wedding is today, because, who knows, it might be!

Jesus, thank you for inviting me to the most glorious wedding celebration of all time. I eagerly await your final return! As I prepare for that day, help me to keep my garments clean through kind words and good deeds. Give me a healthy fear of your power as I prepare to stand in your presence. Help me to draw closer to you as a friend without losing reverence for your holiness. Allow me to see my sin through your eyes and empower me to live a life that honors you and draws others to the celebration that will take place when you return. In your name, Amen.

Personal Reflection

Although many believers regard Revelation as scary and confusing, the book is intended to fortify our faith and give us hope as we await Jesus' return. Therefore, take a few moments to read Revelation 21 in that light. Imagine how you will feel on the day Jesus returns, and thank him for making you spotless and worthy.

Scan the QR code for passages of Scripture

Day 38
Porch Pumpkin

The last couple of weeks, we've been discussing our faith through a wide lens—our salvation through Christ, the redemption of all creation, and eternal life with God. We'll loop back around to that in a couple of days. However, today I want to discuss a more practical aspect of our life and faith.

In a winter devotional, I mentioned the pumpkins that deteriorated into rot on my back porch. Thanks to the kindness of my husband, I was able to harvest a number of seeds before he threw away the goopy mess. As he finished cleaning the porch, I washed my seeds and laid them out to dry, looking forward to planting them in the spring. What I didn't know was that while Wesley scooped the slimy pumpkin remains into trash bags, a few additional seeds fell onto the porch and were subsequently washed into the grass.

Fast forward to spring, I happily planted my seeds in the area of my garden designated for vegetables. For good measure, I also planted a few in pots in case the ones in the ground didn't thrive. The vines were soon flourishing in both locations. To my delight, they were joined by a surprise pumpkin plant where seeds had fallen by my porch. The first porch pumpkin was quickly joined by a second, then a third. Soon, so many new vines began sprouting that I cordoned off the area by my porch as a designated mini-pumpkin patch. In fact, so many pumpkin vines sprouted that I was forced to start pulling them up to make room for my other plants.

The spiritual principle of "sowing seeds" is a sensitive, yet vital aspect of our faith. Although the principle has sometimes been abused by false teachers seeking personal gain, the precept is Scriptural. Paul explains,

> *Remember this—a farmer who plants only a few seeds will get a small crop. But the one who plants generously will get a generous crop. You must each decide in your heart how much to give. And don't give reluctantly or in response to pressure. "For God loves a person who gives cheerfully." And God will generously provide all you need. Then you will always have everything you need and plenty left over to share with others.*
>
> **2 Corinthians 9:6–8**

When we sow into God's kingdom, we open the door for his blessings to flow into our lives. This isn't simply a facile prosperity Gospel premise, but a promise from our Father.

Let's be clear, however, that God nowhere promises that we'll become filthy rich or live a life free of trials. Rather, our Father promises to provide all the resources we need. He also guarantees that our blessings will be abundant enough to share with others.

Before we conclude, allow me to speak frankly for a moment. God can and does bless us in ways that are far more meaningful than monetary gain, yet he also desires to give his children financial security. He doesn't guarantee that we'll become rich simply by "sowing seeds," but when we live according to his statutes, the likelihood of becoming financially secure, emotionally healthy, and mentally stable increases dramatically.

At the core, returning tithes and offerings to God isn't even about money. God owns all the resources in the world, and he doesn't

Day 38

need our money. Tithing isn't truly even "giving" to God since everything we have is a gift from him. Tithes and offerings are an expression of our faith and a posture of our heart. We'll talk more on the topic tomorrow, but for now, let's pray.

Lord, thank you for not only meeting my needs but for pouring out blessings in my life. Teach me to be a joyful and faithful giver. Help me remember that all the resources in the world belong to you, and that all my resources are gifts from you. Teach me to trust you more than my material resources. Give me the courage to return my tithes and offering even when I'm afraid. I desire to reflect your heart by giving generously. In Jesus' name, Amen.

Personal Reflection

Prayerfully evaluate your attitude toward tithes and offerings. What factors have shaped your perspective? Is your approach toward giving grounded in Scripture or based on your opinions and experiences? If you struggle to trust God in this area, ask your Father to grow your faith and show you where you can plant meaningful seeds. Remember that your Father isn't trying to take anything from you, but to give you freedom and flourishing.

_____

_____

_____

_____

_____

Growth, Gardens, & Grace

Day 39
Sowing Seeds

Yesterday we discussed the principle of "sowing seeds" through our tithes and offerings. As the topic is complex, I'd like to spend one more day tilling through some of the nuances. Similar to Paul, Luke teaches, "Give, and you will receive. Your gift will return to you in full—pressed down, shaken together to make room for more, running over, and poured into your lap. The amount you give will determine the amount you get back," (Luke 6:38). Unlike Paul, however, Luke isn't referring to financial investment in God's Kingdom, but to giving forgiveness and grace.

Gifts we return to the Lord should come from every part of our lives. The seeds we sow can be financial or relational. They can be gifts of our time or skills. They can be gifts of kindness, forgiveness, and love.

Although our Father desires that we share our resources generously with all people, he calls us to sow our first seeds close to home. Our primary responsibilities are our family, friends, and home church (1 Timothy 5:8). God calls us to invest in our loved ones and support the local church before we sow seeds abroad. In other words, I would be foolish to plant seeds and tend a garden in my neighbor's yard while neglecting my own. Once we learn to care well for our own seedlings, God can then call us to invest in broader opportunities.

You might be asking, as many people do, "What if the person (or church) in whom I invest misuses my gifts?" I wish I could guarantee that your kindness will never be taken advantage of, nor your financial gifts mishandled. I can't. All I can do is advise you to use discernment, give wisely, and steward carefully. The rest is in God's hands. You aren't responsible for the actions of others, but you *are* responsible for your own obedience to your Father.

Think back to the pumpkin seeds we discussed yesterday. Because I sowed them generously, I reaped abundantly. I could have left them in a jar on my shelf to ensure I would never run out of pumpkin seeds. But why? I would much rather experience the joy of seeing my seedlings sprout and transform into a flourishing pumpkin patch.

Father, thank you for teaching me to trust you more than my material possessions. Show me how I can financially invest in your Kingdom while also sowing seeds of love, kindness, and forgiveness. Open my eyes to opportunities to invest my skills and abilities in your people and your Church. I repent of selfishness, greed, and covetousness. Give me a desire to see the growth of your Kingdom more than my own resources and reputation. Thank you for blessing me abundantly. In Jesus' name, Amen.

Personal Reflection

Look for opportunities to give generously and invest in others today!

Day 39

Day 40
Planted

The last couple of days, we've been discussing seeds. You and I are called to plant seeds with our talents, skills, and resources. In fact, our spiritual rebirth is the fruit of seeds others have planted. Paul describes the process by which we are planted and begin to grow: "Each of us did the work the Lord gave us. I planted the seed in your hearts, and Apollos watered it, but it was God who made it grow," (1 Corinthians 3:5c–6). All of us sow seeds, many of which are cultivated by other people, and all of which are nourished by our Father. Yet, even as we sow seeds, we are continually in the process of being cultivated ourselves.

When we first accept Jesus as Lord, we are planted in him. Paul describes the continuing process of our transformation and maturity: "When you put a seed into the ground, it doesn't grow into a plant unless it dies first. And what you put in the ground is not the plant that will grow, but only a bare seed of wheat or whatever you are planting. Then God gives it the new body he wants it to have. A different plant grows from each kind of seed," (1 Corinthians 15:36b–38). As we commit to live for Jesus and die to self, we become something new and continue growing for the entirety of our lives.

We sometimes view our current, earthly self as unrelated to the person we'll become in eternity. As 1 Corinthians 15 continues, Paul teaches otherwise. He explains,

Day 40

> *Our earthly bodies are planted in the ground when we die, but they will be raised to live forever. Our bodies are buried in brokenness, but they will be raised in glory. They are buried in weakness, but they will be raised in strength. They are buried as natural human bodies, but they will be raised as spiritual bodies. . . . But let me reveal to you a wonderful secret. We will not all die, but we will all be transformed! It will happen in a moment, in the blink of an eye, when the last trumpet is blown. For when the trumpet sounds, those who have died will be raised to live forever. And we who are living will also be transformed. For our dying bodies must be transformed into bodies that will never die; our mortal bodies must be transformed into immortal bodies.*
>
> *1 Corinthians 15:42–44, 51–53*

I don't claim to understand exactly how our present selves are related to our eternal selves or how our current season of growth impacts our eternal state. However, Paul is clear that our present state is the kernel of what we'll become in eternity. Our transformation begins now and continues until our Lord returns to renew all of creation and complete the process. On that day, we can greet him as mighty oaks or wilted saplings. Either way, he will perfect every imperfection and weakness. Yet, when I meet my Lord and Savior, I'd like to stand tall, deeply rooted and flourishing as I welcome him. How about you?

Lord, thank you for offering spiritual rebirth and growth that will continue into eternity. Help me bury my old self and be transformed into your image. Give me the self-discipline to reject the desires of the flesh and, instead, tend the soil of my spiritual growth. I repent of living carelessly and neglecting the health of my soul. Empower me to stand firm upon my faith and become the fully mature and deeply rooted person you've called me to be. As I continue to grow, equip me to sow the seeds of the Gospel in the lives of others. In Jesus' name, Amen.

Personal Reflection

Paul teaches that faith, hope, and love last forever (1 Corinthians 13:13). What seeds are you sowing into lasting personal growth? In what pursuits are you investing your time that will yield eternal benefit? As you reflect, you may want to review your notes from the previous two days.

Day 41
Dandelions

Since we've been discussing the process of sowing seeds the last few days, I thought I would tell you about a crop I sowed long ago. As most children, I didn't know the difference between flowers and weeds. They were all beautiful to me. So, one day, deciding that Pop's grass was woefully lacking in flowers, I decided to sow a crop of dandelions. For what seemed like hours, I searched the front and back yards for dandelion blooms. I picked each one until I was certain I had enough. Not yet knowing about the process of seed growth and germination, I shredded all my dandelions into tiny pieces, expecting that a new flower would grow from each. I then proceeded to methodically spread my "seeds" across every inch of the yard. Proud of my hard work, I sought Pops and Gram to tell them about the exciting surprise that would soon bloom for them.

  At that time, I didn't know dandelions are actually weeds. Most people don't want dandelions in their yard, and my grandparents were no exception. Nonetheless, they gently thanked me, but asked that I refrain from planting more dandelions. I didn't quite understand why they wouldn't want more of the lovely yellow flowers, but I trusted that their knowledge was beyond my own.

  Much later in life, in a reverse set of circumstances, Abel tried to help me in my own garden. Seeing a group of grass-like shoots poking above the mulched bed, he proceeded to uproot each one. After he finished his project, he found me to proudly announce that he'd weeded my garden. Since both of my boys despise pulling weeds, his gesture was amazingly sweet and thoughtful, but I quickly realized that he had uprooted a large patch of gladiola bulbs. Despite my best efforts to replant them, they never recovered from the trauma.

The theological point I am endeavoring to make is that we should ask our Father before making grand gestures on his behalf. No matter how pure our intentions, we simply don't have the wisdom and knowledge of our Father. Isaiah offers the following word of caution from the Lord: "'My thoughts are nothing like your thoughts,' says the Lord. 'And my ways are far beyond anything you could imagine. For just as the heavens are higher than the earth, so my ways are higher than your ways and my thoughts higher than your thoughts,'" (Isaiah 55:8–9). In the light of such knowledge, Solomon offers the following advice: "Trust in the Lord with all your heart; do not depend on your own understanding. Seek his will in all you do, and he will show you which path to take. Don't be impressed with your own wisdom. Instead, fear the Lord and turn away from evil," (Proverbs 3:5–7).

Our Father has knowledge that exists outside of time and space. He sees not only our past, but also our future. His knowledge extends from every hair on our head to every particle of dust in the solar system. Our fleeting, finite knowledge simply can't compare to the wealth of wisdom our Father possesses. This fact, however, shouldn't be cause for frustration because he makes his wisdom available to us! If we simply ask him to guide us and remain humble enough to follow him, he'll lead us exactly where we need to be. Instead of leaning on our own understanding, let's lean on him.

Father, I praise you for your vast wisdom and knowledge. I thank you that, although I am insignificant in the scope of the universe, you love me enough to be intimately involved in my life. I ask you to give me greater wisdom and understanding for your will for my life. I repent of

Day 41

going my own way and ignoring your guidance. Teach me to walk in humility so that I submit to your leadership and walk in the plans you set before me. Help me to turn from evil when it encroaches upon my path and live in holiness so that I can hear your voice clearly. In Jesus name, Amen.

Personal Reflection

Prayerfully meditate on any decisions before you in the coming days, weeks, and months. Make a list of each item in the space provided. No decision is too small to bring before the Lord. Take a few minutes to pray over each item in your list and ask for God to give you clear direction. Ask for the courage to follow even if he leads you in a direction you don't want to go.

_____

_____

_____

_____

_____

_____

_____

_____

_____

_____

Day 42
Walking in Circles

Yesterday we talked about seeking the guidance of the Lord to help us make wise decisions. Today we'll discuss another avenue by which God helps us make wise decisions—wise counsel. But first, I'd like to tell you about army ants.

The name "army ant" actually applies to hundreds of different ant species. They are referred to as army ants because of the way they aggressively band together to search for food. By working together, they can even subdue much larger predators like scorpions and lizards. Their strength in numbers keeps them well provisioned and protected, which is an apt analogy for the benefits of healthy spiritual community. However, being part of the right community is essential.

On some occasions, a group of army ants will become separated from the main party. Without purpose or objective, each ant will simply follow the one in front of it. The small group forms a continuously rotating circle, always walking, but going nowhere. In fact, the ants will continue walking in a circle until they die of exhaustion. Hence, the phenomenon is called a "death spiral."

The aimless ants fittingly illustrate what happens when we align ourselves with the "wrong crowd." Proverbs 13:20 advises, "Walk with the wise and become wise; associate with fools and get in trouble." The people with whom we closely associate impact the person we become and the trajectory of our lives. When we walk with fools, we become more foolish. We live without meaning and purpose,

Day 42

walking in a metaphorical death spiral. Yet, when we walk with the wise, we learn from their wisdom and become spiritually healthy. Instead of trudging in aimless circles, we move forward with purpose.

Although our Father calls us to love all people, he instructs us not to walk with the wicked (Psalm 1:1). As we mature in Christ, we increasingly learn to balance these two aspects of our faith. We can show grace and kindness to even the most unapologetic delinquent while still protecting the integrity of our inner circle of friends and advisors. We can love both the saint and the sinner without following fools into their spiral of destruction.

Father, thank you for placing people in my life who can help me mature and grow. Give me wisdom to recognize the people who will draw me closer to you and the people from whom I should distance myself. Show me how to love every person, yet maintain an inner circle of friends who live with integrity and holiness. Empower me to walk in ways of wisdom and avoid paths that lead to destruction. In Jesus' name, Amen.

Personal Reflection

With whom are you walking today? Are the people by your side following in the steps of Jesus or fumbling through life like a fool? Make a list of 5-10 of the closest people in your life (friends, family, leaders, co-workers, pastors, etc.). Ask God to reveal whether each person is helping you grow in wisdom, spiritual maturity, and health. If you can't answer with an affirmative for any of the people on your list, pray for God to help you set healthy boundaries and relationally distance yourself from that individual. I know the process can be difficult, but your life is too important to waste on walking in circles.

Day 43
Ant Interloper

Since we're on the subject of ants, I'd like to tell you about the fascinating relationship between the alcon blue butterfly and a particular species of red ant. In the larval phase, the alcon blue caterpillars emit a chemical that mimics the odor of the red ant queen. The larvae even emit a high-pitched sound, similar to that which is produced by the queen, to draw the ants' attention. The worker ants, therefore, seek out the larva, transport it to their underground colony, and provide tender care until it pupates.

Although the caterpillar benefits from the relationship, the ant colony faces dire consequences. The parasitic larva will spend up to two years being pampered by the ants and increase in weight by a factor of 100. During that time, the ants will feed the new "queen" at the expense of their own young, experiencing significant population decline as their own offspring die. Only when the larva pupates and emerges as a butterfly do the ants realize their mistake. At that point, however, it's too late to do anything about it. The butterfly, whose body is impervious to ant bites, simply walks out of the nest and flies away.

You and I face an enemy who employs similar tactics. Although the alcon blue caterpillar bears no malicious intent, our enemy desires to steal, kill, and destroy (John 10:10). Paul warns that Satan disguises himself as an angel of light and his followers disguise themselves as servants of righteousness (1 Corinthians 11:14–15). Paul harshly rebukes the Corinthian church for refusing to recognize they were being manipulated, abused, and exploited:

> *You happily put up with whatever anyone tells you, even if they preach a different Jesus than the one we preach, or a different kind of Spirit than the one you received, or a different kind of gospel than the one you believed. . . . After all, you think you are so wise, but you enjoy putting up with fools! You put up with it when someone enslaves you, takes everything you have, takes advantage of you, takes control of everything, and slaps you in the face.*
>
> **1 Corinthians 11:4, 19–20**

Instead of thinking for themselves, the Corinthians were going along with whatever they were told. Instead of evaluating popular beliefs in the light of Scripture, they believed whatever they heard.

Paul's rebuke is just as relevant today as it was nearly 2,000 years ago. The enemy of our souls camouflages himself as a force for good. He'll try to sound like Jesus, smell like Jesus, and look like Jesus. He wants to trick us into inviting him into our lives and homes only to destroy and rob us of everything we hold dear.

Fortunately, God shines a light upon the dark deeds of the Enemy when we seek his illumination. Paul advises, "Carefully determine what pleases the Lord. Take no part in the worthless deeds of evil and darkness; instead, expose them. . . . But their evil intentions will be exposed when the light shines on them, for the light makes everything visible," (Ephesians 5:10–11, 13–14a). Instead of fumbling in the dark and feeding the dysfunction, you and I have the opportunity to expose the lies of the enemy by shining the light of God's truth. Let's continually ask God to light our way and search Scripture for the truth. Only then can we walk in the light and bring his illumination to our world.

Day 43

Lord, thank you for shining your light upon my soul and illuminating the path before me. Give me the wisdom to recognize imposters and false teaching. Help me develop the discipline to immerse myself in prayer and Bible study so that I'm not easily deceived by the enemy. Teach me to recognize the difference between the feel-good-ism of my culture and the truth of your love. Empower me to set healthy boundaries in my own life and erect guardrails against the schemes of the enemy. Show me how to love others unconditionally without enabling or encouraging sin. In Jesus' name, Amen.

Personal Reflection

We are inundated with the popular beliefs of our culture through television, social media, and internet platforms. Meditate on a few social issues near to your heart, and ask God to show you whether your opinions align more with Scripture or popular culture. Then, before you conclude your quiet time for today, memorize the words of Jesus from Matthew 10:16: "Look, I am sending you out as sheep among wolves. So be as shrewd as snakes and harmless as doves." You may want to write or type the verse in a handy place for reference throughout your day.

_____

_____

_____

_____

_____

_____

Growth, Gardens, & Grace

Day 44
Abel's Ant Hill

My son Abel has always been a curious and strong-willed child. I confess, he gets it from me. If you tell us not to do something, we'll only become more interested in doing what you said not to. Such was the state of affairs during one visit to our neighborhood park. As soon as we arrived, I noticed a massive ant hill beyond the perimeter of the playground. Abel, always inquisitive, saw it as well. In response, I issued harsh warnings and stern threats about staying away from the ominous ant volcano.

At the time, both boys were quite young. So, my attention was divided between them, and the moment I began pushing Asher on the swings, Abel scampered to the ant hill. Upon hearing him scream, I turned to see Abel flailing his arms and stomping his feet on top of the ant pile. Already being swarmed and bitten, he was too frantic to even step away from the furious ants.

As any mother would, I rushed to my distressed child, yanked him from the mountain of ants, and began swiping the stinging pests from his body, incurring my own ant bites in the process. Although Abel was far too heavy to be carried, I swept into my arms and began ambling home as quickly as I could. Upon arrival, I disrobed Abel to remove any remaining ants and applied soothing cream to his bites. Fortunately, they weren't severe enough to require a hospital visit.

When I think of Abel's ant pile, I think about the way worry operates. Our Father tells us repeatedly not to worry, and he warns us of the harm it will cause. Then like Abel, we turn around and dash straight into an ant pile of worry. And like Abel's ants, one worry brings hundreds of friends. You see, worry isn't just about one problem. Worry is a state of mind and a position of the heart. When we allow anxious thoughts to creep into our mind, they swarm across our soul, covering us with bites and stings.

Yet, our Father isn't angry when we step into the ant pile of anxiety. He sweeps us into his arms, dusts us off, and comforts us with his love. The psalmist writes, "When my anxious thoughts multiply within my heart, your comfort delights my soul," (Psalm 94:19, my translation). I love this verse because the psalmist is real and honest. In the original Hebrew, he says that anxious thoughts multiply within his *kereb*, a term that refers to the innermost part of a person—the guts, insides, or womb. Although we aren't sure who wrote Psalm 94, the man knew the visceral, gut-wrenching feeling of worry. Yet, he had also intimately experienced God's grace. When he speaks of God's comfort, he uses the term *tanhum*, which stems from the idea of deep breathing and physical soothing.[5] The same word is used in Isaiah 66:13 to compare God's consolation to that of a mother comforting a child. In addition to soothing, the term *tanhum* also carries the nuance of encouragement, hope, and joy. Our Father not only soothes our soul, but gives us hope for the future.

Our psalmist was familiar with the crushing, paralyzing weight of worry, but he also knew that our Father is both compassionate and strong enough to lift the oppressive burden from our heart. In their younger years, when my boys felt anxious and overwhelmed, I would hold them in my arms, speak soothing words, take deep breaths, and encourage them to breathe deeply with me. I imagine our Father doing the

---

[5] Marvin R. Wilson, "*nacham*," *Theological Wordbook of the Old Testament*, ed. R. Laird Harris, Gleason L. Archer Jr., and Bruce K. Waltke (Chicago: Moody Press, 1999), 570.

Day 44

same for us. What a beautiful picture. Let's relax into his embrace, take a deep breath, entrust him with our cares, and move forward with hope!

Father, thank you for bringing comfort to my soul, peace to my mind, and calm to my body. Teach me to trust you more and grow in my faith. I repent of doubting you and trying to face my worries alone. Help me replace anxious thoughts with the truth of your Word before my worries have an opportunity to multiply. I ask you to fill me with a joy that overflows and give me opportunities to share the reason for my hope. In Jesus' name, Amen.

Personal Reflection

During the first several devotionals this volume, we discussed strategies for managing worry and stress. Revisit your notes from days two, three, and four. Prayerfully meditate on whether you have made any progress. Have you adopted and maintained any strategies that have helped? Did you start strong and then forget to maintain your proactive measures for managing stress? What strategies might you need to revisit to help you continue to grow in this area? Write your thoughts below.

_____

_____

_____

_____

_____

_____

Day 45
Asher's Pet

Since I told you about Abel's ant pile yesterday, I thought I would tell you about Asher's "pet worm" today. He found the worm one morning when we were playing outside. Initially, I thought he was playing with an imaginary worm since Asher has never been a kid who enjoyed creepy-crawlies. Plus, I couldn't see any worm in his hands from where I was sitting with Abel, who was a baby at that time.

Shortly thereafter, we decided to go back inside for a snack. Asher asked if he could bring his pet worm inside, and I gave assent, still thinking the worm was imaginary. As we entered the kitchen, Asher walked straight to the table and placed his worm upon it. To my absolute and utter horror, I discovered that Asher had adopted a pet maggot. Faster than the speed of light, I disposed of the disgusting creature and wiped Asher's hands with a disinfectant. I then proceeded to sanitize every square inch of my kitchen. In case you were wondering, I never discovered where Asher had found the rogue maggot.

I wonder if God feels the way I felt at that moment when we sin against him. I was revolted to see my precious boy handling the disgusting larvae. God, similarly, sees the true nature of our sin. While we dabble in disobedience and experiment with vice, our Father agonizes over the filth with which we dirty ourselves. We are simply too immature and ignorant to understand we're playing with maggots.

Some people view the persona of God in the Old Testament as judgmental and cruel—a much different God than the one we know from the New Testament. To the contrary, however, God saw the full extent of human depravity, and through the people of Israel began the process of redeeming us. He commanded his people to be set apart so that they would be a light to the nations around them, but to shine that light, Israel would first have to learn to live differently. In Leviticus 20:22–23, God commanded, "You are therefore to keep all My statutes and all My ordinances, and do them, so that the land to which I am bringing you to live will not vomit you out. Furthermore, you shall not follow the customs of the nation which I am going to drive out before you, because they did all these things; therefore I have felt disgust for them." Lest you think God's disgust is overly harsh, you should know that the peoples surrounding Israel regularly participated in cultic practices that included child sacrifice and abhorrent sexual rites. I would be more upset if God *wasn't* appalled by that.

Yet, we serve a good Father who extends grace and mercy beyond our capacity for imagining. Moses records the self-description of God, "Yahweh! The Lord! The God of compassion and mercy! I am slow to anger and filled with unfailing love and faithfulness. I lavish unfailing love to a thousand generations. I forgive iniquity, rebellion, and sin," (Exodus 34:6–7a). Only through God's limitless grace can the vileness of our sin be forgiven. Therefore, even when we don't understand his commands, even when our sin doesn't seem so bad, even when we can't see any harm in a little illicit fun, we simply can't see the whole picture. Next time you are tempted, remember Asher's maggot and ask yourself if you really want to pick that nasty thing up.

Father, thank you for your compassion, mercy, and unfailing love. Forgive me for abusing your grace as a license to sin. Open my eyes to the gravity of sin. I ask you to make it just as repugnant to me as it is to you. Give me the self-discipline to walk in integrity and holiness. I ask you to remove my sinful desires and empower me to overcome temptation. In Jesus' name, Amen.

Day 45

Personal Reflection

Prayerfully reflect on your own tendencies and temptations. Are you tolerating any disobedience in your life simply because it seems like a "little" sin? Are you dabbling with any temptations because they seem harmless? Ask God to help you see your infractions through his eyes so that they would become offensive rather than appealing to you.

Day 46
The Weight of the World

Since we spent some time in Exodus and Leviticus yesterday, I thought we would stay in the early books of the Bible for another day and continue our discussion of sin. Rebellion against God isn't simply an offense against him. God calls us to a life of obedience because he wants to protect his children. In addition to real-world consequences, sin creates a spiritual, mental, and emotional burden on our souls. Rebellion against God is simply a weight we were never meant to bear.

The heaviness of sin becomes starkly apparent in the narrative of Cain and Abel. In Genesis 4:6–7, after Cain becomes angry at his brother, the Lord asks him, "Why are you angry, and why has your face fallen? If you do the right thing, will your countenance not lift? But if you don't do the right thing, sin is crouching at the door. It desires to dominate you, but you must master it," (my translation). As we all know, Cain did not master his sin. He shortly murdered his brother and bore the consequences. In Genesis 4:13, the bereft brother cries out to God, "My sin is too great to bear!" (my translation).

In the original Hebrew, the brilliant author exposes a clear contrast between the lightness of obedience and the burden of sin. Cain could choose to lift (*nasah*) his spirits if he did the right thing or he could sin and bear (*nasah*) the heavy guilt and consequences. In simpler terms, the weight of obedience is light, but the weight of rebellion is unbearably heavy.

Day 46

Have you ever lifted something heavy? I'm sure you have. The heaviest items I tend to lift are bags of dirt and mulch for my garden. As much as I love gardening, those bags are hard to carry! They are unwieldy, often damp, and hard to grip. Each bag is too large to carry in my hands, but if I hoist it onto my shoulder, my whole body is off balance. If I try to drag it, the bag rips open and makes a huge mess.

Perhaps transporting dirt and mulch isn't a regular activity for you, but we've all carried something heavy and unwieldy before. Perhaps you've moved into a new home and experienced the challenge of moving heavy furniture through small doorways. Even carrying our kids can be a challenge sometimes. When Abel was a toddler, it was nearly impossible to carry him somewhere he didn't want to go.

I hope you see my point. Sin is a heavier burden than any physical weight we might carry. The reason disobedience feels so unwieldy, uncomfortable, or even excruciating is because God never intended for us to bear the weight of rebellion against him. Although we will never be perfect, we can choose more wisely than Cain. Instead of hoisting the weight of sin, guilt, and shame onto our shoulders, let's uplift the countenance of our lives through faithful obedience.

Father, thank you for providing safe guidelines in which I can live and thrive. Teach me to view your commandments as a blessing rather than a burden. I repent of disobedience in thought, words, and deed. Give me the self-control and determination to overcome every temptation. When sin crouches at my door, empower me to keep the door firmly shut. I ask you to reveal any hidden sins in my life of which I'm unaware. Thank you for sending Jesus to bear the weight of my sin so that I can walk with a joyful countenance and lightness of heart. In Jesus' name, Amen.

Personal Reflection

Are any past or present sins weighing heavily upon your soul? The process of freedom from sin and shame can be a lengthy process, but the best time to start is now! Over the next three days, we'll discuss steps and strategies for overcoming sin and releasing our burdens to the Lord.

- First, begin with worship, praise, and thanksgiving. Express gratitude to Jesus for sacrificing himself so you can receive freedom and forgiveness. Thank God for his goodness and grace. You may even want to spend time listening to or singing along with worship music.
- Second, repent of any known sin in your life. Make a list below and ask God to take away your desire to rebel against him in that area. If you are uncomfortable writing down specifics, you can write vague statements that only you understand. (If you aren't aware of any disobedience in your life, pray for God to reveal any sins of which you are unaware.)
- Third, repent of any past sins for which you still feel guilt or shame. Add these to your list.
- Fourth, pray and thank Jesus *aloud* for bearing your guilt, shame, and punishment. Thank him for healing your heart and forgiving your offense. Commit to leave your sin, guilt, and shame at the cross. Even if your emotions don't yet align, even if you don't *feel* guilt-free, continue confessing this truth!

_____

_____

_____

Day 46

Day 47
Bearing the Name

The last couple of days we've been discussing the weight of sin in our lives. Sin is heavy because rebellion against God is a burden we were never intended to bear. However, sin has been part of our reality since the fall of Adam and Eve. Thankfully, our Father has a plan to lift the burden of sin from our shoulders.

As I mentioned a couple of days ago, God began the process of redemption through the line of Abraham and the people of Israel. God called Israel to be a people set apart from the nations—a holy people who could teach other nations about the Father. God proclaimed to his people, "You will be my kingdom of priests, my holy nation," (Exodus 19:6). The Lord then proceeded to outline a list of guiding principles, otherwise known as the Ten Commandments.

The third commandment, in particular, is relevant to our current discussion. As the most misunderstood of the ten, the commandment is usually understood as a prohibition against taking the Lord's name "in vain." In other words, if we can refrain from using curse words involving the name of God, we'll have mastered this command. Sadly, such an understanding completely misses the deep theological significance of the third commandment.

If you'll allow me to dive deep once more today, I'd like to draw your attention to the original Hebrew. Literally translated, the verse reads, "You shall not bear (*nasah*) the name of the Lord your

Day 47

God in vain," (Exodus 20:7).[6] Such few words hold great depth of meaning! First, I want to point out that the phrase "bearing my name in vain" shouldn't be understood as prohibition against cursing, but as a statement of undesirable outcome. God was saying, "Don't bear my name with futility—don't represent me in such a way that you fail to show the world who I am."

Second, I want to draw your attention to the term *nasah*, "to bear." I hope you recognize the word from yesterday, but I'll recap just in case you don't. God implored Cain to live righteously so that his countenance would be lifted up (*nasah*), but Cain instead chose to disobey God and bear (*nasah*) the weight of his sin. Thousands of years later, Israel was offered the same choice. Would they submit to the Lord, bear his name, and become a nation of priests or continue to bear the burden of sin? Although the correct choice seems obvious, they didn't always choose wisely. The people of Israel struggled with their choice, just as we struggle today. We'll continue the story tomorrow, but for now, let's pause and reflect.

Father, thank you for allowing me, like the people of Israel, to bear your name. Empower me to represent you well among my peers. Equip me with the knowledge and resources I need to overcome sin and guilt so that I can make you known to the world. Help me discover the root causes of my disobedience and shame so that I can uproot them and move forward in freedom. Teach me to discern truth from deception as I seek to better understand who you are and who you've created me to be. In Jesus' name, Amen.

---

[6] I am indebted to Carmen Imes for this translation insight and highly recommend her book *Bearing God's Name* (IVP Academic, 2019).

Personal Reflection

Let's continue working toward freeing ourselves from the burden of sin and guilt as we add to the steps we began yesterday.

- First, begin again with worship, praise, and thanksgiving. Then, if God has brought any additional areas of sin or shame to your awareness, add them to your list from yesterday.
- Second, prayerfully review your notes from yesterday and look for patterns. Are there any recurring situations in which you tend to disobey your Father? Do certain circumstances trigger rebellion or laxity in your spiritual walk? Do certain circumstances dredge up guilt and shame from the past? Do you tend to disregard God's commands when you're with certain people? What else can you learn from your lists? Write down your thoughts.
- Third, ask God to show you the "why" of your tendencies. Think about when each rebellious pattern of behavior began to emerge. Why did you react the way you did? What need were you seeking to fulfill? What fallacies were you, and might you still be, believing about yourself? Why might you feel shame or guilt in certain situations or around certain people?
- Fourth, close again by thanking Jesus for removing the burden of sin from your heart

_____

_____

_____

_____

_____

Day 47

Day 48
Bearing Bricks

Over the last few days, we've been discussing the burden of sin upon our souls and the blessing of bearing God's name. Although sin isn't the most *fun* topic to discuss, it is an issue that impacts the entire tenor of our lives. Bearing God's name with holiness brings joy to our hearts and lightness to our souls, while carrying the weight of sin is a nearly unbearable burden.

As we closed yesterday, we considered whether Israel would accept God's offer to bear his name in holiness or, like Cain, choose to bear the burden of sin. To the extent that we are able, let's consider how the concept of bearing or carrying something might have sounded to the Israelites. When God asked Israel to bear his name, they had just emerged from slavery. In Exodus 1:13–14, Moses records, "the Egyptians worked the people of Israel without mercy. They made their lives bitter, forcing them to mix mortar and make bricks and do all the work in the fields. They were ruthless in all their demands." For approximately 400 years, Israel had borne the burden of forced labor and brutal overlords.

Although we, as modern believers, often view the Old Testament commands as harsh and cumbersome, God's Law was a blessing to Israel. Instead of bearing bricks for evil masters, they could choose to bear the name of the compassionate God who had rescued them from slavery. The choice seems obvious, but sadly, it wasn't. As Pharaoh pursued the escaping Israelites, fear overtook their fledgling faith.

Day 48

> *They cried out to the Lord, and they said to Moses, "Why did you bring us out here to die in the wilderness? Weren't there enough graves for us in Egypt? What have you done to us? Why did you make us leave Egypt? Didn't we tell you this would happen while we were still in Egypt? We said, 'Leave us alone! Let us be slaves to the Egyptians. It's better to be a slave in Egypt than a corpse in the wilderness!'"*
>
> **Exodus 14:10b–12**

Then again as Israel approached the Promised Land, they doubted God's ability to protect his people and fulfill his promise. Upon the spies' return from their reconnaissance, the people of Israel descended into panic. Moses records,

> *Then the whole community began weeping aloud, and they cried all night. Their voices rose in a great chorus of protest against Moses and Aaron. "If only we had died in Egypt, or even here in the wilderness!" they complained. "Why is the Lord taking us to this country only to have us die in battle? Our wives and our little ones will be carried off as plunder! Wouldn't it be better for us to return to Egypt?" Then they plotted among themselves, "Let's choose a new leader and go back to Egypt!"*
>
> **Numbers 14:1–4**

The lack of faith exhibited by the Israelites is heartbreaking. Nearly every member of the community preferred burdens that were back-breakingly heavy because their old ways of life were familiar. The people were so afraid to trust God and submit to his lordship that they clung to their oppression like a security blanket.

Choosing slavery over trusting God sounds like a ridiculous decision, but don't we do the same? When you and I cling to our sin, we are acting like the Israelites, seeking slavery because it is comfortable and familiar. Our Savior, however, implores us to relinquish our burdens to him. In Matthew 11:28–30, Jesus says, "Come to me, all of you who are weary and carry heavy burdens, and I will give you rest. Take my yoke upon you. Let me teach you, because I am humble and gentle at heart, and you will find rest for your souls. For my yoke is easy to bear, and the burden I give you is light."

Before we enter our time of reflection for today, soak up the words of Jesus and thank him for bearing your burdens at the cross and for continuing to lift them up every day since.

Jesus, I thank you, once again, for bearing the weight of my sin, guilt, and shame. Thank you for teaching me to walk in your ways and live in freedom. As I seek to live in greater obedience, give me insight into past wounds that continue to have an impact on the present. Grant me greater spiritual discernment so that I can identify unhealthy patterns and situations in my life. Teach me to walk in greater holiness so that I can better bear your name to those who don't know you. In your name, Amen.

Personal Reflection

Although today is the final day we will discuss freedom from sin and guilt, I pray these final few steps will propel you toward continued freedom, healing, and holiness.

- First, begin again with worship, praise, and thanksgiving.
- Second, prayerfully review your notes from yesterday and consider what new insights you've learned about God or

Day 48

yourself. Perhaps you identified a need that you've been seeking to fill with empty substitutes. Perhaps you identified a falsehood you've been believing about yourself or your Father. Ask God to give you discernment as you examine yourself and your tendencies. Identify 2–3 key insights and write them down.

- Third, begin to realign your thoughts and actions in accordance with God's Word. Replace any false beliefs with the truth and replace transgressions with new behaviors. Avoid situations in which you tend to sin or feel shame and replace them with settings that help you grow healthier.
- Fourth, and possibly the most vital step of all, entrust your burdens to a friend, spiritual leader, and/or professional counselor. Trusted friends and advisors can help us see past our own blind spots and provide accountability when we are weak. Write down a few possible names below and ask God in whom he would have you confide.

_____

_____

_____

_____

_____

_____

_____

_____

Day 49
Rest

Yesterday, we closed with Matthew 11:28–30, a beautiful passage in which our Savior promises to lift our burdens and provide rest. A couple of days ago I also compared the weight of sin and guilt with the heavy, unwieldy bags of dirt and mulch I use in the garden. What relief I feel when Wesley, Asher, and Abel take the bags and carry them for me! I can continue to enjoy my favorite aspects of gardening without needing to bear the heavy burdens around the yard. Jesus, likewise, bears our burdens so that we can live a joyful life filled with meaning and purpose.

We've spent several days talking about the manner in which God gives us rest from the heavy burden of sin and guilt. Jesus, however, lifts burdens that go far beyond those which are caused by our rebellion. In this life, we often face trials that are completely beyond our control and struggles through no fault of our own. Sometimes, we simply need Jesus to provide rest when our souls become weary from the frenetic pace of our lives.

Throughout the biblical narrative, the concept of rest crops up at key points. First, we know that God created the universe in six days then rested on the seventh day. Much later, when God brought the Israelites out of Egypt, he promised to give them rest. Even later, the authors of the New Testament promised a permanent rest that is yet to come. According to Hebrews 4:9–10, "there is a special rest still waiting for the people of God. For all who have entered into

God's rest have rested from their labors, just as God did after creating the world."

So, what is biblical rest, and what is the "special rest" upon which we still wait? Let me assure you that God's rest is even better than a nap on the couch or a day on the beach. Although we typically envision rest as a cessation of activity, biblical rest is anything but. When God rested on the seventh day, he didn't lay down and take a nap. Likewise, when Jesus promises us rest, he isn't offering a soak in the hot tub.

Let me paint a biblical picture of rest. When the author of Genesis reports that God rested, he is telling us that the Father was free to enjoy his creation. God had fulfilled his responsibilities as Creator. He could spend time interacting with creation and caring for its creatures. The rest Jesus offers points back toward that first state of perfect rest. Our Savior offers rest from sin, guilt, shame, worry, and fear, grief—all the burdens that we carry through life. Jesus provides rest for our *souls*, and in doing so, he equips us to spread the Gospel, serve one another, and persevere through persecution. That hardly sounds restful, but when our souls are at rest, the "burden" of bearing God to the world isn't a burden at all.

As we enjoy our present state of rest, we also look forward to a future rest. Like God's perfect rest on the seventh day of creation, we look forward to the permanent rest we'll receive when we will have fulfilled our present responsibilities, and we will be able to spend eternity enjoying the presence of God with the people that we love. There will be no more war, conflict, sin, sadness, poverty, oppression, or death!

In the meantime, how can we enjoy our present rest? As we've discussed the last several days, seeking to eliminate sin provides rest for our burdened souls. Not simply avoiding sin, however, but drawing ever closer to our Savior brings great rest and relief. As we accept

Day 49

more of his yoke, seek his will, and become more like him our burdens grow ever lighter. How will you seek Jesus' rest today?

Jesus, thank you for offering rest for my soul now and an even more perfect rest in the future. I want to experience more of the rest that you offer today. Help me lay my burdens at your feet and pick up faith and holiness in increasing measures. Help me to obey you so that I'm not weighed down by selfish desires or disobedience. Reveal specific ways that I can grow more like you and walk more fully in your rest. Help me to be an agent of reconciliation of this earth and offer your rest to others. In your Name, Amen.

Personal Reflection

Ask Jesus to show you at least one practical way you can foster a greater degree of his rest in your life. Do you need to continue working through the process of freedom from sin and guilt? Do you need to be more intentional about your prayer and devotional time? Do you need to cultivate the fruit of the Spirit in your life? Do you need to entrust Jesus with a specific worry? Do you need to set aside an actual day of Sabbath rest in your week? Decide on at least one action step and implement it this week.

_____

_____

_____

_____

_____

Growth, Gardens, & Grace

Day 50
Confused Cardinals

We've dealt with heavy topics the last few days. Today, we'll lighten the mood and, fittingly, discuss airy creatures. I've introduced my beautiful bluebirds already. Now let me tell you about my confused cardinals. You see, cardinals aren't the smartest of birds. In fact, they are one of the least intelligent bird species. As I explained in the winter volume of *Rooted and Flourishing*, birds sometimes fly into windows, failing to notice the clear glass. Most species of bird will learn from their mistake, but not cardinals. They'll fly into the same window over and over again. I don't know if they're hoping for a different outcome or if they've simply forgotten what will happen.

One spring, a whole flock of cardinals became enamored with my front porch window. From inside the house, we would hear thump after thump. I'd go outside and scatter the birds away, but they would return within minutes. I put stickers all over the window and set plants in front of it. Nothing seemed to deter the persistent birds, who continued flinging themselves at my window for weeks.

Like the cardinals, you and I sometimes become confused. Although Christ transforms our mind when we accept his lordship, we tend to revert to old behaviors and patterns of thinking. Paul warns us about the danger of an unkempt soul, "With the Lord's authority I say this: Live no longer as the Gentiles do, for they are hopelessly confused. Their minds are full of darkness; they wander far from the life God gives because they have closed their minds and hardened their hearts against him," (Ephesians 4:17–18). A more literal translation of the passage reveals that living and thinking like the world isn't simply confusing, it's futile.

Thankfully, none of my cardinals died, at least not on my porch, but I would guess that a few incurred brain damage or other injuries from the repeated trauma. Similarly, living and thinking according to the standards of the world is like beating our head against the wall (or window). Such behavior is not only meaningless and futile, but harmful. Why would we foster futility when our Father promises an abundant life full of meaning and joy?

Father, thank you for transforming my mind so that I can live with meaning, purpose, and joy. Forgive me for wasting my time and energy on futile pursuits. Teach me to focus my mind upon things that honor you and diligently walk in holiness. Give me compassion for those whose minds are darkened and confused, and provide opportunities for me to share the Gospel. In Jesus' name, Amen.

Personal Reflection

Prayerfully meditate about whether you are tolerating any futile thoughts or behaviors. Ask God to show you situations in which you tend to act or think in meaningless, irrational, or hurtful ways.

_____

_____

_____

_____

_____

Day 50

Day 51
Building on the Bush

As I mentioned yesterday, cardinals aren't the smartest birds. In addition to bashing themselves against my windows repeatedly, they also lack the innate sense to build their nests in safe places. I recently observed this phenomenon when a pair of cardinals built their nest in one of my bushes. The bush wasn't especially stable, nor was the nest high off the ground, i.e., safe from dogs.

As the weeks passed, the birds laid eggs, and the hatchlings emerged. I anxiously watched the attentive parents fly to and fro, feeding their babies. I began to hope that the nest was sturdier than I'd thought and that the family of cardinals would thrive. Yet, my hopes were dashed one day when I walked through the yard and saw a lifeless baby bird in the grass.

Over the course of the next few days, I found the remainder of the hatchlings, and the nest itself, on the ground. I surmised that a strong wind had blown the birds and their home asunder. Sadly, the mother and father of the chicks continued to fly around the bush frantically, as if searching for their nest full of hatchlings.

In Matthew 7:24–27, Jesus teaches about the importance of building upon stable foundations.

> *Anyone who listens to my teaching and follows it is wise, like a person who builds a house on solid rock. Though the rain comes in torrents and the floodwaters*

Day 51

> *rise and the winds beat against that house, it won't collapse because it is built on bedrock. But anyone who hears my teaching and doesn't obey it is foolish, like a person who builds a house on sand. When the rains and floods come and the winds beat against that house, it will collapse with a mighty crash.*
>
> **Matthew 7:24–27**

When we build our lives on Christ's teaching, we create a safe and stable foundation from which we can withstand trials. Our wise preparation also creates a barrier of protection in which our loved ones can shelter. Conversely, ignoring the teaching of our Lord keeps us in a precarious position from which we can be blown into oblivion. When we deny the Lordship of Jesus, we create an environment so unstable that our entire life can collapse. Even worse, just as the adult cardinals failed to create a safe nest in which to raise their offspring, our unwise planning can hurt those we love the most.

Rather than haphazardly assembling our lives on the sandy shore or the billowy bush, let's build on the bedrock of our Savior.

Lord, thank you for providing instructions regarding how to live wisely. Give me the foresight and faith to build my life upon your teaching. Expose any areas of instability in my foundation and teach me to shore up those weak areas. Help me rest in the safety of your love and protect my own loved ones as I live out your principles. I repent of foolish decisions I've made in the past and commit to learn from them. In Jesus' name, Amen.

Personal Reflection

Prayerfully reflect on your foundations. Does your security rest in status, success, or finances? Is your faith predicated upon the

Growth, Gardens, & Grace

absence of trials? Does your trust in God depend upon getting your way? Alternately, is your faith rooted in his goodness, justice, and wisdom no matter the circumstance? As you meditate and pray, ask your Father to fortify your foundation with faultless faith. Write down your thoughts so you can refer back to them tomorrow.

Day 52
Building A Blueprint

Yesterday we discussed fortifying our foundations. Like my cardinals building their nest on an unstable bush, we often root our faith in faulty assumptions about God. Just as the bush was a poor substitute for an actual tree, mistaken beliefs about our Father and his Kingdom are a dangerous substitute for grounded faith.

In order to ground our lives in the stability of God's truth, our greatest resource is Scripture. Throughout the Bible, God reveals who he is, who he has created us to be, and how he has called us to live. The Sermon on the Mount, in particular, offers a blueprint for a life of faultless faith. Although we may never attain the fullness of Jesus' standards, each step of obedience fortifies our foundation.

Instead of focusing on my words today, I'd like you to spend time reading those of Jesus. You'll first read the Sermon on the Mount and then work on your own blueprint. Even if you already have a deeply rooted relationship with Jesus, evaluate the structural integrity of your faith. To give you time to meditate and self-reflect, my comments today are intentionally brief.

Lord, thank you for loving me enough to provide stable foundations upon which I can build my life. Forgive me for trusting my own wisdom and desiring my own will more than yours. As I study your word and seek your presence, I pray you will fortify my foundations. Teach me to have an unshakable faith from which I navigate life with joy and resilience. Give me opportunities to reach out and help others find their own foundation of faith. In Jesus' name, Amen.

Personal Reflection

Prayerfully read Matthew 5–7 and meditate on the extent to which your foundation reflects the one outlined by Jesus. Review your notes from yesterday and pray for God to show you any areas in which your foundation is unsteady. In the space provided, write down opportunities to build upon your blueprint—at least one for the present, one for the next 6 months, and one for the next year.

Scan the QR code for passages of Scripture

_____

_____

_____

_____

_____

_____

_____

_____

Day 52

Day 53
Apple Trees

The first few years we lived in our current home, I had two apple trees growing in the backyard. Each year, as they began to bloom, I would eagerly anticipate the fresh, homegrown fruit that would soon grow. As the apples ripened, Asher and Abel would help me pick them, then we would enjoy making applesauce, apple strudel, and apple pie together.

One year, I noticed that some of the leaves on the tree had black spots. I'm not an expert with fruit trees, but I knew black spots were a bad sign. Thus, I immediately bought a spray that was supposed to cure fruit tree diseases and set out to save my tree. I sprayed it diligently and still harvested a good crop of apples.

Despite my best efforts, however, the trees continued to worsen. Each year, I harvested fewer apples, and the fruit that did grow was small and deformed. Finally, I reached the difficult decision that the trees had to be cut down.

My ill-fated experience with apple trees reminds me of Paul's teaching about leaven. The apostle warns, "Don't you know that a little leaven leavens the whole dough? Clean out the old leaven so that you may be a new batch, since you are, in fact, 'unleavened,'" (1 Corinthians 5:6–7, my translation). Paul cautions us about the dangers of false teaching. Just as a tiny bit of leaven will cause an entire loaf of bread to rise, the smallest lie can impact the entire course of our lives. Like the tiny black spots that spread and destroyed both of my apple

Day 53

trees, believing the lies of the Enemy can have devastating consequences.

Through Scripture, we learn the truth about God, ourselves, and our world. Yet, we are constantly inundated with "truths" about the world around us. We are even told to "live our own truth" as if the truth were a subjective reality that we have the liberty to create. Even the teachings of Scripture are often twisted into ugly parodies of the actual truth.

Thankfully, our Father has given us the undiluted truth through Scripture and in the person of our Savior, Jesus! When we accept the truth of Christ, we become "unleavened" through our experience of his grace.

Paul, however, warns us to remain on our guard. To use his metaphor, leaven is all around us. We are like dough-balls, and if we aren't careful, that leaven will stick to us and get mixed into our lives. Our Father will never abandon us or cut us down like my apple trees, but getting that leaven out will take a lot of work. Let's follow Paul's advice and keep that old leaven out of our hearts.

Jesus, thank you for showing me the truth about God, about myself, and about your creation. Help me be diligent to study your Word so that I can discern the truth from the lies of the Enemy. Teach me to remain on guard so that I can never be deceived. When I hear others proclaim your Word, give me a healthy desire to confirm the truth through my own studies. In your name, Amen.

Personal Reflection

Prayerfully evaluate your own Bible study habits. Do you, like the Bereans of Acts 17:11, examine the Scriptures daily to see if the teachings you hear are true? Or do you only sporadically study God's Word?

Ask God to show you one step you can take to deepen your study of his Word and gain a greater understanding of his truth. If you aren't sure where to start, ask a spiritual mentor or pastor for guidance.

Day 54
Hunting Buddies — Part 1

In addition to birds, many random creatures make their way into my yard. The nearby pond serves as an inviting water source that draws animals to our property. Throughout the year, we'll encounter standard neighborhood chipmunks and squirrels. We'll also host snakes, mice, rats, moles, rabbits, turtles, and even deer. Although I don't wish harm on the animals, I don't want them digging in my yard or dining in my garden.

That's where my dogs enter the picture. Smokey and Pepper, my jumbo mini-schnauzers, work together to keep the yard free of pests. They'll stalk and corner prey from opposite directions to increase their effectiveness. When successful, they bring their trophies to the patio to show off their hunting prowess.

In addition to hunting partners, Smokey and Pepper are siblings and best friends. They play together, nap together, guard each other, and protect their territory. They aggressively bark at any human or animal that gets near their house or their people. They also keep each other clean with regular eye and ear cleanings, which is kind of gross.

Smokey and Pepper illustrate the power of working together. Like my dogs, we can partner to protect one another and accomplish God's purposes, a principle clearly stated in Scripture:

> *Two people are better off than one, for they can help each other succeed. If one person falls, the other can*

reach out and help. But someone who falls alone is in real trouble. Likewise, two people lying close together can keep each other warm. But how can one be warm alone? A person standing alone can be attacked and defeated, but two can stand back-to-back and conquer. Three are even better, for a triple-braided cord is not easily broken.

Ecclesiastes 4:9-12

When we work together, we are unstoppable. When we do life alone, we are vulnerable. We all need someone to help us up when we stumble and fall. We need someone to lean on when we are weak.

For well-rounded relational health, each of us needs three types of relationships. First, we all need a mentor—someone who can guide us and help us grow in maturity. Second, we need friends—people with whom we can share our deepest secrets and struggles. Third, we need to support other people, which is deeply fulfilling and necessary for our own growth.

Relationships come more easily to some people than others, but everyone needs relationships. No matter whether you prefer being alone or being with people, relationships are a vital aspect of spiritual health. Just as important, when we work together, God can use us to build his Kingdom and spread the Gospel. Unlike my dogs, who join forces to kill backyard invaders, you and I get to bring the gift of life in Christ!

Lord, thank you for planting me in the midst of people who care for me. Help me be humble enough to receive guidance and selfless enough to strengthen others. Reveal how I can more effectively develop relationships with a church family and share the Gospel with the world. Lead me to the right people who will help me grow in my faith. In Jesus' name, Amen.

Day 54

Personal Reflection

Identify at least three people in your life who fulfill the relationship types we discussed: mentor, friend, and mentee. If you don't have strong relationships in each category, ask God to reveal the right people.

Day 55
Hunting Buddies — Part 2

Yesterday we discussed the importance of fostering different types of relationships. Just as my dogs work together to defend their territory, protect each other, and guard our family, the body of Christ is most productive and effective when we work together.

The battle between the armies of Amalek and Israel serves as an excellent illustration of God's people working together to support one another, protect one another, and achieve success.

> *So Joshua did what Moses had commanded and fought the army of Amalek. Meanwhile, Moses, Aaron, and Hur climbed to the top of a nearby hill. As long as Moses held up the staff in his hand, the Israelites had the advantage. But whenever he dropped his hand, the Amalekites gained the advantage. Moses' arms soon became so tired he could no longer hold them up. So Aaron and Hur found a stone for him to sit on. Then they stood on each side of Moses, holding up his hands. So his hands held steady until sunset. As a result, Joshua overwhelmed the army of Amalek in battle.*
>
> **Exodus 17:10–13**

Day 55

The army of Israel achieved victory because of their coordination and cooperation. They were able to win the battle because they had fostered intentional relationships of support within the community *before* the conflict took place.

As mentioned yesterday, we need three types of relationships, each of which is modeled in the life of Moses. First, we all need a mentor, as Jethro was to Moses. Shortly after Israel's battle with Amalek, Jethro, Moses' father-in-law visited the encampment of Israel. He celebrated Moses' success and applauded his skillful leadership. Yet, Jethro also offered wise leadership counsel and continuing mentorship (Exodus 18).

Peer relationships are also vital. Like Aaron and Hur holding up Moses' arms, we need people who will stand by our side. Friends enrich our life because they celebrate our success and support us through struggles.

Finally, we should guide and support others. Just as Jethro mentored Moses, Moses likewise mentored Joshua. Moses not only taught Joshua to lead with confidence and wisdom, but set the entire nation on a trajectory for success by equipping a strong leader to follow in his footsteps.

You and I can accomplish exponentially more when we learn from mentors, lean on friends, and establish spiritual successors. As we partner through community, we not only spread the Gospel more effectively, but enjoy the love and support of our family of faith.

Lord, thank you for resourcing me to learn and grow. Open my eyes to opportunities to be a supportive friend, serve as a mentor, and learn from my leaders. Forgive me for trying to do everything on my own instead of leaning on the people you've placed in my life. Show me how I can more effectively develop meaningful relationships that foster both personal and Kingdom growth. In Jesus' name, Amen.

Personal Reflection

Yesterday, I asked you to identify at least three people in your life who fulfill the three relationship types we discussed. If you are lacking in any of the three categories, prayerfully consider reaching out to initiate a new relationship today. If you have strong relationships in all three areas, reach out to your mentor, friend, or mentee with words of gratitude, support, or encouragement.

_____

_____

_____

_____

_____

_____

_____

_____

_____

_____

_____

_____

Day 56
A Cord of Three Strands

The last couple of days, we've been discussing the importance of fostering meaningful relationships—a vital aspect of our spiritual growth. We've already looked at Ecclesiastes 4:9-12, but I want to draw your attention back to verse 12: "A person standing alone can be attacked and defeated, but two can stand back-to-back and conquer. Three are even better, for a triple-braided cord is not easily broken." Together, we can be more productive, we can help each other through hard times, we can provide for each other's needs, and we can protect each other. Indeed, a cord of three strands is not easily broken.

This truth comes alive for me in my garden. I use rope for various purposes. I create make-shift trellises out of rope. I use it to stabilize tall plants, trees, and bushes. At one point, Wesley even used rope to hold our old lawn-mower together.

If you look closely at rope, you'll see that the cord is typically composed of three strands. If you look more closely, you might see that each strand is composed of three smaller strands, and each of those is composed of even smaller strands. Why is the rope constructed this way? The numerous strands make the rope stronger! If one of the individual strands grows weak, gets snagged, or breaks, the other strands will keep the weaker strands from falling apart. What an empowering metaphor for the body of Christ!

We still have to be on guard, however. At one point, as I was tying off a rope in my garden, the strands literally came apart in my hands. The cord had been left in the elements, and because it hadn't been given proper care, the filaments grew weak. A similar principle applies in our relationships. In Colossians 3:13-15, Paul describes how to care for the relational ties that bind us together. The apostle instructs,

> *Make allowance for each other's faults, and forgive anyone who offends you. Remember, the Lord forgave you, so you must forgive others. Above all, clothe yourselves with love, which binds us all together in perfect harmony. And let the peace that comes from Christ rule in your hearts. For as members of one body you are called to live in peace. And always be thankful.*
>
> ***Colossians 3:13–15***

In case you missed it, *love* is the agent that binds our strands together. From love then flows other vital elements of our fellowship, such as forgiveness, peace, and gratitude.

When our individual filaments are bound by love, grace, harmony, and thanksgiving, our entire body is stronger. As God's people, we form a beautiful and indestructible tapestry. If you are feeling frayed, you can rely upon the filaments around you to uphold and sustain you. Or if you are winning at life, you can provide the strength and support that those around you need. Either way, simply don't do life alone.

Lord, thank you for placing people in my life who will support me when I am weak. Allow me to likewise support others who need love and encouragement. Forgive me for isolating myself during times of struggle, and forgive me for neglecting those who need support during my seasons of strength. Help me to pour love, forgiveness, peace, and gratitude into the people in my life. Allow me to be a conduit of your grace as I seek to strengthen the body of Christ. In Jesus' name, Amen.

Day 56

Personal Reflection

Take some time today to care for your relational bonds. If you are feeling weak, worried, or anxious, confess your struggles to a trusted friend and ask them to pray for you. If you are feeling joyful and strong, ask God to show you who you can encourage today.

Day 57
Green Thumb

I imagine you know a few people who can claim a "green thumb." Other people facetiously boast of a "black thumb," implying that they kill everything they try to grow. This mystical attribute makes it sound like the universe endows some of us with the power to grow plants, while depriving other people of the same skill. In reality, however, being a successful gardener requires hard work and intentionality, as we've discussed the last several days. Just like any endeavor at which we hope to succeed, we must hone our craft and gather knowledge. So, over the years, I've learned about different types of soils, different types of lighting, different types of plants, and so much more.

For example, each species of plant has different needs in order to flourish. Succulents enjoy sunshine, sandy soil, and dry conditions. Ferns typically require shade, rich soil, and ample moisture. Yet, even within the fern and succulent species, individual subtypes have different needs. Although my string of pearls is a succulent, it thrives best when I water it frequently. My ostrich ferns could not be killed by an atomic bomb and thrive in any conditions. In sum, I've spent countless hours learning what each plant needs and creating the right conditions in which it can flourish.

To a much greater degree than plants, each human has distinct characteristics and needs. Paul understood the necessity of customizing our interactions accordingly and modeled a life of strategic evangelism. He writes,

Day 57

Even though I am a free man with no master, I have become a slave to all people to bring many to Christ. When I was with the Jews, I lived like a Jew to bring the Jews to Christ. When I was with those who follow the Jewish law, I too lived under that law. Even though I am not subject to the law, I did this so I could bring to Christ those who are under the law. When I am with the Gentiles who do not follow the Jewish law, I too live apart from that law so I can bring them to Christ. But I do not ignore the law of God; I obey the law of Christ. When I am with those who are weak, I share their weakness, for I want to bring the weak to Christ. Yes, I try to find common ground with everyone, doing everything I can to save some. I do everything to spread the Good News and share in its blessings.

1 Corinthians 9:19–23

As he spread the Gospel across a region with dramatic cultural and racial diversity, Paul made sure to understand the people to whom he ministered and foster connections with them, often at great personal expense.

Whether we are called to plant churches, preach sermons, teach Bible studies, or none of the above, we are all called to share the Good News of God's love. Following in the footsteps of our Savior and the example of Paul, the Gospel involves bold action and personal sacrifice. Building connection and trust with others might require a sacrifice of time, convenience, and personal preference. When we meet people where they are, there is simply no shortcut to getting there.

Perhaps you have a metaphorical "black thumb" when it comes to sharing the Gospel. Maybe you are awkward or nervous, and you don't know what to say. Maybe you don't feel like you are intelligent enough or holy enough to represent Jesus. First, let me assure you that we all start somewhere. When I accepted Christ, I was uncomfortable even saying the words "God" or "Jesus." Second, simply being kind speaks more loudly of God's love than any theological presentation. Third, consider whether your Father might be calling you to seek mentoring relationships with people who can help you hone your skills and grow in knowledge. We'll talk more about that tomorrow, but for now, let's pray.

Father, thank you for creating each of your children beautifully unique. Teach me to see the value in every person and have greater compassion toward each individual. Guide me as I seek to extend kindness and foster connections with those who don't know you. Give me spiritual discernment to understand how to share your love in a way it can be received. Empower me to set aside my own desires, conveniences, and preferences in order to meet people where they are and lead them to you. In Jesus' name, Amen.

Personal Reflection

Today or in the near future, make an intentional effort to connect with someone in your life who doesn't know Jesus. Simply be kind, spend time talking, ask questions, and get to know them better.

_____

_____

_____

Day 57

Day 58
Master Gardener

Yesterday we discussed making connections in order to share God's love more effectively. I realize that personal evangelism can be an uncomfortable pursuit for many believers. However, we aren't trying to convert people into a crazy cult, we're sharing the best news in human history. God has granted us the blessing of bearing the best gift anyone could ever receive!

You may have heard that religion is not a topic for polite conversation. I fully agree. No one wants religion shoved in their face. The Gospel message, however, isn't about religion. It's about our Father's unconditional love, forgiveness, and freedom. So, if the idea of evangelism sends you into a nervous sweat, just think of it as telling people about your Dad, whose name happens to be Yahweh, and your best friend, whose name happens to be Jesus.

More importantly, if we take steps to equip ourselves, we remove much of the fear factor from talking about our faith. As we closed yesterday, I mentioned that mentoring relationships can help us hone our skills. This is true of any field. In regard to gardening, I've never taken any classes or certifications, but I know someone who has. My mom is a master gardener. who completed a whole series of courses for her certification. She routinely gives me gardening advice, and I know that if I have a question, I can go to her.

Similarly, you don't need a theological degree or pastoral title to share the Gospel effectively. You can, however, hone your skills by

Day 58

seeking guidance from someone in that category. According to Hebrews Heb 13:7, "Remember your leaders who taught you the word of God. Think of all the good that has come from their lives, and follow the example of their faith." The disciples had Jesus, Timothy had Paul, Joshua had Moses. Every one of us should have someone who refines us and helps us grow. Who is that person for you?

Father, thank you for giving me a wonderful message of hope and love to share. Show me what steps I need to take in order to better equip myself to share the Good News effectively. Help me be diligent to pursue mentorship and learn from those with more experience. Give me confidence in ever increasing measures as I tell people about you. In Jesus' name, Amen.

Personal Reflection

Consider whether you have someone in your life who can help you become a more effective disciple of Christ. If you don't, ask God to show you who you might ask to mentor and guide you. If you already have someone, ask him or her to help you determine one way you can become a more effective sharer of the Gospel message.

_____

_____

_____

_____

_____

_____

_____

Growth, Gardens, & Grace

Day 59
Dry Creek Bed — Part 1

One of the reasons we chose our current home many years ago was the potential I saw in the landscaping. The curving flower beds, raised planters, and variety of trees were already lovely, if a bit overgrown and patchy. I knew that I could build upon the existing terrain to create a stunning garden.

As we settled into our new home, I worked with feverish joy on my new garden. On three sides of the house, the landscaping transformed and thrived, just as I'd planned. The fourth side, however, simply wouldn't cooperate. My raised beds looked okay and the variety of bushes were healthy, but no grass would grow because of the deep shade. The whole area was dominated by red Alabama dirt. When it rained, the red dirt would even splash up and stain the side of the house.

I decided that an entirely new strategy would be required if I ever wanted that side of my home to look appealing, and I began to consider the idea of a dry creek bed. Knowing I would require his help, I discussed the idea with Wesley, and he responded favorably.

I began the project by outlining the borders of my future creek bed with a shovel, starting at our driveway and winding into the back yard. Then we began to dig, and dig, and dig some more. For months, we toiled in the hard red clay, spending more time and effort than we'd ever imagined would be required.

I'll tell you the rest of the story tomorrow, but let me pause to make a point. Like my patch of lifeless red dirt, we've all been spiritually barren at some point in the past. Our mistakes dirtied the landscape of our lives worse than the red mud splashed on my house. Our old ways of living became so unappealing that something had to change. Fortunately, our Father took the initiative to create a beautiful haven for our souls. We didn't even have to dig, toil, or work for it. In terms of my dry creek bed, it would be as if I simply walked out of my house to find the entire project complete without having to lift a shovel. Paul describes this generous gift of God in his letter to Titus.

> *Once we, too, were foolish and disobedient. We were misled and became slaves to many lusts and pleasures. Our lives were full of evil and envy, and we hated each other. But—When God our Savior revealed his kindness and love, he saved us, not because of the righteous things we had done, but because of his mercy. He washed away our sins, giving us a new birth and new life through the Holy Spirit. He generously poured out the Spirit upon us through Jesus Christ our Savior. Because of his grace he made us right in his sight and gave us confidence that we will inherit eternal life.*
>
> **Titus 3:3–7**

Out of his limitless mercy, our Father brings life to the dry, barren ground of our souls. He washes away our sin more completely than a pressure washer takes the stain of red clay off my bricks.

Paul explains that once our Father gives us life and cleans us up, we can walk in confidence. So, my question to you is—Are you walking in the confidence of your salvation? In the day-to-day grind of life,

Day 59

we sometimes forget about the miraculous transformation that has taken place in our lives. We forget just how dry and barren the terrain of our souls used to be. Today, let's remember God's great mercy, walk in confidence, and enjoy the healthy new growth that has taken place in our souls.

Father, thank you for bringing life to my soul and joy to my heart. Thank you for your limitless love and mercy. Help me live with a heart full of gratitude for the transformation you effected in my life. Empower me to walk in the confidence of my salvation as I continue to grow in my faith. Give me opportunities to share the reason for my hope and joy. In Jesus' name, Amen.

Personal Reflection

Today, seek to walk in confident faith. Be mindful of the healthy places in your soul and the lovely parts of your life, and thank God at every opportunity.

Day 60
Dry Creek Bed — Part 2

Yesterday we discussed God's gift of new life through which he transforms our souls into a thriving landscape. Our Father asks nothing in return, and we don't have to toil or strive to experience the beautiful gift of our new life. I can't say the same about my dry creek bed.

As I mentioned yesterday, I wanted to transform a barren area in my yard by replacing the lifeless dirt with a dry creek bed—basically a creek filled with rocks instead of water. To create the rock feature, we first had to dig the trench, a slow and tedious process since red Alabama dirt is basically clay. So Wesley, myself, Asher, and Abel dug in with not only shovels, but also pickaxes.

In the beginning, we were sustained by the excitement of a new project. After a while, however, the boys' willingness to help was exhausted. I didn't feel right about forcing them to dig, so Wesley and I continued on our own. As we dug, we piled the dense clay along the curb, hoping and praying that the regular yard waste services would remove it.

As the weeks passed, the curb dirt piled up, and the yard increasingly looked like a war zone. I began to doubt we had the ability to bring my vision to life, and thought despairingly, "What have we done?" The neighbors even looked concerned. As people walked their dogs, I could see them casting nervous glances at the carnage of my yard. A few neighbors were even bold enough to ask, "What are you doing?," always with a nervous chuckle. I would assure them, with much greater confidence than I felt, that we were creating a new garden feature that would be stunning once complete.

I wasn't sure I believed my own words, but at that point, turning back wasn't an option. The only way out was to continue digging through. Even when the digging was finished, however, our work was far from complete. We purchased four tons of river rock, which were promptly delivered on pallets. Shovel by shovel, through sunshine and rain, we deposited the rocks into the crevasse we had dug. Yet, still the project was incomplete.

Although we had displaced much of the lifeless red dirt, my creek was still surrounded by it. Thus, I spent a few more weeks tilling the hard dirt, while mixing in rich black soil and compost. A trip to my parents' lake house provided the finishing touches for our project. With the help of my mom, we filled buckets with ferns and other shade-loving woodland plants, with which I surrounded my creek.

And just like that, we were finally finished! The city waste department even picked up our extra dirt! Though the project had required more work than I'd ever dreamed, the end result was likewise more beautiful than I'd imagined. The lush woodland landscape was worth every drop of sweat and second of work.

When I think about the transformation of my barren dirt into a flourishing garden, I think of Isaiah 61. In this passage, which I frequently pray over my own life, the prophet says:

The Spirit of the Sovereign Lord is upon me,
for the Lord has anointed me
to bring good news to the poor.
He has sent me to comfort the brokenhearted
and to proclaim that captives will be released
and prisoners will be freed.
He has sent me to tell those who mourn

Day 60

> *that the time of the Lord's favor has come,*
> *and with it, the day of God's anger against their enemies.*
> *To all who mourn in Israel,*
> *he will give a crown of beauty for ashes,*
> *a joyous blessing instead of mourning,*
> *festive praise instead of despair.*
> *In their righteousness, they will be like great oaks*
> *that the Lord has planted for his own glory.*
>
> ***Isaiah 61:1–3***

Just as God transforms the barrenness of our own souls, he equips us to be the means by which he brings life to others. Because we were once barren, we can personally attest to God's free gift of new life.

Yet, the free gift of new life we received wasn't truly free. Jesus purchased our salvation with his literal blood, sweat, and tears. As his followers, we are called to follow in his cruciform pattern of selfless love. We are called to dig trenches and build bridges in order to reach those who are lost in the wilderness. Like my dry creek bed, the effort may be more than we expect, but the result will be more beautiful than we can imagine!

Father, thank you for the saints who came before me and shared your message of hope and freedom. Empower me to likewise bear your Good News to those who don't know you. Give me the courage to live in the light of the Gospel and speak of my faith boldly. Forgive me for remaining silent in moments when I should speak out or take action on your behalf. Strengthen my heart and my hands as I work to create opportunities for people to encounter you. Thank you for the opportunity to share the best news the world has ever received. In Jesus' name, Amen.

Personal Reflection

A few days ago, I encouraged you to make an intentional effort to connect with someone in your life who doesn't know Jesus. Find another opportunity to chat with the same individual and tell them about how Jesus has changed your life and your heart. If you've never shared your personal testimony before, write it below (or type it for easier editing), then practice sharing it with a spiritual mentor.

_____

_____

_____

_____

_____

_____

_____

_____

_____

_____

_____

_____

_____

Day 61
Spring Cleaning

Spring is a season of bustling activity in my garden. Much preparation is required for the garden to grow and thrive in the coming months. I have to clear away old, dead foliage to make room for new growth. I till the soil and plant seeds for summer vegetables. In my pots and baskets, I add fertilizer or replace the soil entirely. The plants that have wintered inside the house, I gradually transition back into the sunshine with increasing periods of time on the patio each day. I won't bore you with a comprehensive list of my spring gardening tasks. My point is that intentional effort is required to cultivate and maintain a healthy garden.

We discussed yesterday that God freely gives us new life, which transforms our souls into flourishing gardens. However, we must maintain our garden with intention and care if we desire a healthy spiritual life. Just as my garden won't magically sustain favorable conditions for growth, we can't grow spiritually without creating conditions in which growth can occur.

Peter teaches that getting rid of harmful behavior primes the soul of our soul for nourishment and growth. He advises, "So get rid of all evil behavior. Be done with all deceit, hypocrisy, jealousy, and all unkind speech. Like newborn babies, you must crave pure spiritual milk so that you will grow into a full experience of salvation. Cry out for this nourishment," (1 Peter 2:1–2). Eliminating deceit, hypocrisy, jealousy, slander, and other destructive habits is like clearing away the old dead foliage in my garden. Removing the dead plant matter allows the new plants to establish roots in the soil and extend leaves toward the sun. Growth can still occur even if I don't clear away the dead foliage, but the process is slower and the plants will be a stunted, and sub-par version of what they could have been.

We'll continue studying this passage tomorrow, but I want to make one further point today. The condition of our spiritual life dictates the tenor of every other part of our life. Thus, if we desire a life of purpose, meaning, and joy, we must tend the garden of our soul. The work isn't always easy or fun, and growth doesn't happen overnight. However, a deeply rooted and flourishing life in the Lord is worth every second of exertion we invest.

Lord, thank you for freeing me from bondage to evil thoughts and behaviors. Help me put away my old habits so that I can cultivate healthy new growth. I repent of allowing deceit, hypocrisy, jealousy, and slander to clutter the garden of my soul. Reveal any other past patterns of thought or behavior that are impeding my growth. Give me a greater desire to nourish my soul and grow toward maturity. In Jesus' name, Amen.

Personal Reflection

Prayerfully reflect on the list of old, dead behaviors that Peter lists: deceit, hypocrisy, jealousy, and unkind speech. Ask God to reveal whether any of these patterns of thought or behavior might be impeding your growth. If more than one is cluttering your garden, ask God to show you which one he would have you work on clearing away first.

Day 61

Day 62
A Healthy Diet

Yesterday we discussed preparing the garden of our soul for growth. Just as I clear the old, dead foliage from my garden in the spring, Peter advises us to remove destructive thoughts and behaviors from our life in order to grow. The apostle says, "So get rid of all evil behavior. Be done with all deceit, hypocrisy, jealousy, and all unkind speech. Like newborn babies, you must crave pure spiritual milk so that you will grow into a full experience of salvation. Cry out for this nourishment," (1 Peter 2:1–2). Getting rid of old, hurtful tendencies clears the way for us to receive God's nourishment and flourish without impediment.

Just as clearing our spiritual clutter requires purposeful action, we must likewise intentionally seek God's nourishment. In fact, Peter says to crave it like a baby craves milk. Have you ever experienced a hungry baby? Babies literally kick and scream because they want their meal so badly. They can't be consoled or distracted until their hunger is satisfied. That's how intensely we should desire God. We should be so laser focused on seeking his nourishment that nothing takes higher priority and nothing can deter us from getting it.

Yet, even if we don't quite meet Peter's hungry baby standard, we can strive for it. We might not always *feel* like praying, studying, and obeying God, but we can discipline ourselves to do it anyway. Just as I don't always enjoy clearing away dead foliage or fertilizing my plants, tending the garden of the soul isn't always fun. In both scenarios, however, I know that I will reap the benefits of a beautiful garden.

Day 62

The bottom line is that we will never "grow into a full experience of salvation" if our only nourishment is one hour of church per week or a few sporadic prayers. If we are, however, intentional to consume the right spiritual nutrients in sufficient quantities, our roots will grow deep and our branches will reach high.

Although each of us might need a slightly different spiritual diet, allow me to suggest a few staples. Weekly church services, although not sufficient alone, are necessary for spiritual growth. Sunday worship offers a healthy meal of essential nutrients: worship, prayer, community, and Bible study. These same elements, we also need on an every-day basis, and just as we wouldn't skip a day without eating food, we shouldn't neglect our spiritual nutrition.

A multitude of other elements contribute to a healthy diet, such as fasting, service, meditation, accountability, and tithing. God has more than enough victuals to satisfy even the deepest hunger. So, how does your spiritual diet look? Are you feasting on God's nourishment or is your plate full of junk?

Lord, thank you for providing all the nutrients I need to grow into a healthy, mature believer. Teach me to cultivate a healthy diet and give me the discipline to maintain it. Forgive me for subsisting on junk food instead of seeking the pure nourishment you offer. Give me a greater desire to dine upon your Word and drink in your presence. Place a hunger in my heart for meaningful community. Help me be more intentional about taking time to worship you both corporately and privately. In Jesus' name, Amen.

Personal Reflection

Consider your spiritual diet over the previous 7 days. Write each day (Monday–Sunday) below and beside each list the spiritual nutrients you dined upon each day (to the best of your memory). Once complete, prayerfully reflect upon the nutritional value of your diet. Just as you selected one behavior to rid yourself of yesterday, prayerfully select one way you can make your diet healthier today.

Day 63
Surprise Sprouts

The last few days, we've been talking about gardening and growth. Just as tending to our literal garden facilitates growth, we must likewise cultivate the garden of our soul if we desire spiritual growth.

Early each spring, I clear the old, dead foliage from my garden, nourish the soil with fertilizer, plant seeds, and spread mulch, in addition to a myriad of other tasks. Once the garden begins to grow, I revel in watching my plants emerge and flourish. I get even more excited about what I refer to as "surprise plants," ones that grow in unexpected places through no effort on my part. For example, tomato plants occasionally sprout in random locations throughout the yard, probably from seeds distributed by birds. Impatiens (colorful shade-loving flowers) crop up literally everywhere due to seed pods that explode each fall. A few impatiens even started growing in my houseplants. I have no idea how that happened! Alternately, a large patch of houseplants, alocasia, once started growing outside beside my porch. At the time, I didn't even own that type of plant.

My point is that when we create the right conditions for growth, growth naturally occurs. We might experience growth in the places we've carefully cultivated and tended, but we might also grow in unexpected places and unexpected ways. We might experience personal growth inside our souls while also seeing sprouts emerge in others.

John rejoiced when the seeds he planted sprouted and flourished. As he corresponded with his friend Gaius, he expressed great joy over hearing the news. John writes, "Dear friend, I hope all is well with you and that you are as healthy in body as you are strong in spirit. Some of the traveling teachers recently returned and made me very happy by telling me about your faithfulness and that you are living according to the truth. I could have no greater joy than to hear that my children are following the truth," (3 John 1:2–5). John had tended his garden well, created conditions for growth, and reaped a harvest of blessing for himself, his friend Gaius, and the entire community to which Gaius ministered.

Let me reiterate that the growth we experience isn't always the growth for which we plan. Some of the churches in whom Paul invested his time, Corinth in particular, caused him more grief than joy. Yet, the lack of desired outcome doesn't invalidate the process of cultivation (2 Cor 2:1–4). I would venture to say that even in his frustration with Corinth, Paul learned how to be a more effective evangelist and church planter. Certainly, the church afforded him an opportunity to grow in patience and perseverance.

I've experienced similar seasons in my ministry during which I carefully planted seeds and nourished the soul of another, only to watch them pour gasoline on their spiritual garden and light it on fire. Although those individuals didn't grow as I hoped, I grew more wise and discerning as a pastor.

So, keep tending to your spiritual garden. Clean out that which is dead, nourish your soil, and start planting seeds. Watch for seedlings to emerge and flourish in your own heart and in those you love. If you don't immediately see the growth you expect, widen your field of vision and look for unexpected sprouts in unexpected places.

Father, thank you for nourishing me and helping me grow. Teach me to be diligent in tending the garden of my soul. Help me trust you with the result. I repent of becoming frustrated with you when my growth doesn't

Day 63

happen when, where, or how I expect. Give me greater discernment so that I can recognize growth even in unexpected places. In Jesus' name, Amen.

Personal Reflection

Think about a time when you endeavored to grow in some area of your life, but were disappointed or frustrated when you didn't achieve the desired result. Reevaluate the experience, widen your field of vision, and identify how you grew or helped others grow.

_____

_____

_____

_____

_____

_____

_____

_____

_____

_____

_____

_____

Day 64
Just a Little Patience

Over the last couple of days, we've been talking about how to prepare the garden of our soul for optimal growth. As we already discussed, Peter gives us much advice on how to grow. In the second of his letters, the apostle offers further instructions. He exhorts,

> *By his divine power, God has given us everything we need for living a godly life. We have received all of this by coming to know him, the one who called us to himself by means of his marvelous glory and excellence. And because of his glory and excellence, he has given us great and precious promises. These are the promises that enable you to share his divine nature and escape the world's corruption caused by human desires. In view of all this, make every effort to respond to God's promises. Supplement your faith with a generous provision of moral excellence, and moral excellence with knowledge, and knowledge with self-control, and self-control with patient endurance, and patient endurance with godliness, and godliness with brotherly affection, and brotherly affection with love for everyone. The more you grow like this, the more*

Day 64

> *productive and useful you will be in your knowledge of our Lord Jesus Christ.*
> **2 Peter 1:3–8**

In short, the more intentional our preparation for growth, the greater growth we will experience, and the more fruit we will bear.

In particular, the growth strategy I'd like to highlight today is patient endurance. We all know that growth doesn't happen overnight. When I sow seeds, they might take weeks to sprout and months to grow into fully mature plants. Some seeds grow more quickly and some grow more slowly. Some plants grow so quickly that I can scarcely keep them contained to the spot I want them. Some plants grow so slowly that they take all spring *and* summer to fully develop.

Spiritual growth exhibits a similarly uneven growth timeline. In some seasons of life, growth comes easily, and we bear abundant fruit. In other seasons, growth takes place so slowly that we can't even detect its occurrence. Alternately, some people are better equipped to grow quickly. Perhaps their souls were well tended and nourished as a child, creating optimal conditions for flourishing. Other people, perhaps having grown up in trauma, must exert a greater amount of effort in their spiritual gardens to create growth and reap a harvest.

Whatever your growth looks like, however, continue cultivating with patient endurance. Even if your spiritual growth is so slow that it's nearly imperceptible, remember the encouragement of Paul: "At just the right time we will reap a harvest of blessing if we don't give up," (Galatians 6:9b).

Lord, thank you for extending endless patience toward me. Help me to become more like you and grow in patient endurance. Empower me to persevere even when my efforts seem to produce no fruit. Teach me to live with integrity, self-control, and love even when I don't feel like it. Equip me to take steps toward growth every single day, no matter what is going on in my life. Give me greater discernment to understand how I'm growing, even in seasons of slow growth. In Jesus' name, Amen.

Personal Reflection

Re-read verses 5–7 of Peter's exhortation above. Prayerfully choose one strategy Peter suggests for growth. Practice it throughout your day in conjunction with patient endurance.

Day 65
Finicky Ferns

Today we'll talk once more about tending to the garden of our soul. Over the last few days we've discussed optimal conditions for growth. Yet, how do we respond when our efforts don't provide the results we expect? What should we do when the garden we diligently nurture produces scrawny, lackluster fruit? As we discussed yesterday, we can cultivate patient endurance. We can also, however, take proactive steps.

Let me illustrate by telling you about my ferns. I have more than 10 different types of fern. I'm fascinated by their variety of colors, shapes, and patterns. My hardy outdoor ostrich ferns thrive along one entire side of my house. I'm fairly certain an atomic bomb couldn't kill them. On the opposite side of the house, I have several ghost ferns with delicate mint and purple colored leaves. These are a favorite snack for the rabbits, much to my despair.

My indoor and patio ferns are a source of even greater emotional turmoil. Since they can't survive outdoors in winter, I keep them in pots and carefully tend them year round. These potted ferns are less common, quite beautiful, and very finicky. If they don't get just the right amount of light and water, the beautiful fronds quickly wither and die. When this happens, I don't blame the fern. I know I must identify the problem and find a solution.

Likewise, our process of growth may stutter and stumble at times. Due to our innate instinct for self-defense, we tend to blame external factors, such as our peers, location, or circumstances.

However, just as blaming my ferns won't create conditions for growth and health, blaming external elements won't equip me to find a solution.

In truth, external circumstances could be impeding our growth, but we must move beyond them and look for solutions. The author of Proverbs lauds the virtue of seeking wisdom: "Let the wise listen to these proverbs and become even wiser. Let those with understanding receive guidance by exploring the meaning in these proverbs and parables, the words of the wise and their riddles. . . . For simpletons turn away from me—to death. Fools are destroyed by their own complacency," (Proverbs 1:5–6, 32). Due to the poetic nature of Proverbs, the advice being offered here may seem slightly confusing, so let me clarify: seek the wisdom of scripture, dig into God's Word, and allow it to shape your life. Be intentional, be proactive, and refuse to become complacent. We must allow Scripture to shine a light on any impediments to growth and illuminate any issues within our hearts.

If we honestly determine, with the Holy Spirit's help, that our failure to flourish isn't a result of our own patterns of thought, speech, or behavior, we can look outward. Yet even at that point, we don't cast blame and give up. We continue to seek wisdom and explore solutions. If you'll allow me to be transparent, however, years of ministry have taught me that the obstacles to growth are almost always inside our own hearts. So, next time the garden of your soul is looking a bit withered, consider how you might refine your gardening techniques.

Father, thank you for providing wisdom for real life in your Word. Give me the self-discipline to seek your guidance continually. Search my heart and reveal any internal issues that are impeding my growth. Grow my capacity for discernment so that I can readily identify both internal and external obstacles. Teach me to make wise decisions that draw me closer to you and equip me to grow. Empower me to seek solutions rather than blaming circumstances. In Jesus' name, Amen.

Day 65

Personal Reflection

Today, I'd like you to think through an exercise called "stop-start-continue." Since we're using gardening analogies, we'll call it "uproot-plant-maintain." Prayerfully consider your own growth trajectory, and determine one area of life that you should uproot. This isn't necessarily something sinful, although it could be. You may simply need to uproot something that no longer contributes to your growth. Next, what seeds should you plant to foster future growth and flourishing? Finally, what current habit is helping you grow? How can you maintain this area of your garden to ensure it continues to bear fruit?

Day 66
True Love

In several earlier devotionals, I shared about my grandparents, especially my Pops. Today, I'd like to tell you more about Gram and the unlikely circumstances of her marriage to Pops.

Pops was a poor boy from Illinois, but Gram was a genteel Texas rose. The youngest of four siblings, Gram had one older sister and two older brothers. Her father was a Methodist minister, and while the family wasn't wealthy, their congregations provided well for them.

When Pops came back from the war, he was stationed in San Antonio. At the time, Gram was just finishing nursing school in the same city. When they met, as Gram told me many years later, Pops was walking with a cane in his hand (from war injuries) and a flask of whiskey in his pocket. Nicknamed "Slick," Pops was quite the bad-boy, especially for a pampered preacher's daughter.

As the young couple began to date, fall in love, and talk about marriage, Gram's family became concerned. One of her older brothers even wrote a letter to Pops, telling him that he wasn't good enough for his sister, and that if he truly cared for her, he would leave her alone. Unsure whether her family would support their union, therefore, Gram and Pops eloped. Although they would soon reconcile with her family, the surprise union was shocking and heartbreaking, especially for Gram's father, who had hoped to marry his daughter.

Gram had known full well how her decision would impact her father and her family, but she did it anyway. Why? Because her love for Pops was so great that she was willing to risk everything to be with him. In Scripture, Jesus teaches that this is the type of love we should have for him. Luke records, "A large crowd was following Jesus. He turned around and said to them, 'If you want to be my disciple, you must, by comparison, hate everyone else—your father and mother, wife and children, brothers and sisters—yes, even your own life. Otherwise, you cannot be my disciple,'" (Luke 14:25). For you and I, as the bride of Christ, nothing should be more important than our devotion to Jesus. Neither family, nor friend, nor job, nor hobby, nor anything else in this world should come before our commitment to our Lord. If that sounds extreme—it is! Jesus gave everything, including his very life, on our behalf. The least we can do is give our lives in return.

Jesus, thank you for sacrificing your life so that I can experience the forgiveness and freedom of my Father. Forgive me for allowing my priorities to become disordered and for neglecting my relationship with you. Give me the self-discipline and perseverance to relinquish anything that I've been putting ahead of you. Rekindle my love and my desire to serve you. In your name, Amen.

Personal Reflection

Prayerfully consider your priorities. Are you careful to ensure that nothing gets in the way of your quiet time with the Lord? Do you allow any relationships or activities to interfere with your capacity to serve him? Ask God to rekindle your love for him and seek opportunities to prioritize your relationship with him this week.

_____

_____

Growth, Gardens, & Grace

Day 67
Holiday Inn

Gram and Pops had a long, happy marriage, despite the misgivings of Gram's family. They spent the early years of their marriage in Texas, later moving to his home town in Illinois, and eventually landing in Alabama due to a work transfer. Pops provided well for his family as he rose to upper management in a large chemical manufacturing plant.

As a child, I traveled with them often to visit our extended family in Texas. The car ride was a long, two-day day trip that involved an overnight stay somewhere en route. Although Pops was no longer a poor boy, he was extremely frugal, so the lodgings he chose were somewhat less than five-star. As for me, I didn't care where we stayed, but I always crossed my fingers for a swimming pool.

One trip stands out in my memory because Gram and Pops rarely quarreled, at least in front of me. As we approached the end of our first day on the road, Gram suggested that we stay at a Holiday Inn. The well-known chain would be a substantial upgrade from our usual lodgings, and it was certain to have a pool. Pops summarily dismissed the suggestion and continued searching for a more economical locale. Gram decided to press the issue, but Pops continued to refuse. Becoming increasingly frustrated, Gram finally shouted, "We can afford to stay at the Holiday Inn!" I wisely kept my mouth shut and my opinion to myself, especially when we checked into a hotel that was *not* the Holiday Inn.

Although uncomfortable at the time, I recall the memory with warmth. Despite their disagreement, Pops and Gram were both frugal and wise with their finances. I learned much from their example, and this was one of my first lessons on money management. Gram and Pops lived humbly and simply because it gave them freedom. They were free to travel, free of debt, and free from pride. They weren't concerned with impressing others, including Gram's successful older brothers, one a wealthy physician and the other an esteemed biology professor.

In my eyes, Gram and Pops lived out Hebrews 13:5–6:

Don't love money; be satisfied with what you have.
For God has said,
"I will never fail you.
I will never abandon you."
So we can say with confidence,
"The Lord is my helper,
so I will have no fear.
What can mere people do to me?"
Hebrews 13:5–6

My grandparents were satisfied and secure. They lived wisely and enjoyed the gifts God blessed them with rather than coveting the riches of others or competing for status.

Gram and Pops, and my parents as well, set an example for which I'm forever grateful. Through their humility and frugality, I learned that the desire for more stuff, status, and money is an unquenchable thirst. As the Lord says to Judah through the prophet Haggai: "You have planted much but harvest little. You eat but are not satisfied. You drink but are still thirsty. You put on clothes but cannot keep warm. Your wages disappear as though you were putting them in pockets

Day 67

filled with holes!" (Haggai 1:6). We can only truly be content when we appreciate the gifts God has provided and manage them well.

Wealth isn't inherently good or evil. Our response to it however, will either take us down a path of futility or freedom. I know which one I prefer!

Lord, thank you for generously providing everything I need. Help me recognize the abundance of resources you place at my disposal and use them wisely. I repent of craving wealth and status while neglecting to appreciate your blessings. Teach me to exercise discipline in my spending habits so that I can live free of debt and better utilize my resources in your service. Help me root my self-worth in your love rather than my car, house, job title, or bank account. Make my heart humbler so that I can better reflect the image of my Savior. In Jesus' name, Amen.

Personal Reflection

Prayerfully meditate upon your attitude toward status and wealth. Do your spending habits reflect wisdom and humility or excess and pride? Are you managing your resources well or sinking further into debt? If your finances are massively out of order, consider asking a fiscally wise friend to help you determine what steps might be needed to correct course. Otherwise, ask God to show you at least one step you can take to manage your resources more wisely.

_____

_____

_____

_____

Growth, Gardens, & Grace

Day 68
Popularity Contest

Some people will do almost anything to become famous. Reality shows are proof that humans crave the spotlight. On a smaller scale, many of us desire promotion, prestige, and popularity. Even in the context of the church, many believers hope to achieve a place of prominence. In a healthy heart, this desire simply reflects the God-given motivation to reach our full potential and honor him with our gifts. In an unhealthy heart, this desire stems from a desire to become more powerful, prosperous, and important than one's peers. In reality, most of us fall somewhere between these two poles.

As someone who enjoys the spotlight, I've always been careful to ensure my motivation to teach, preach, and write remains pure and healthy. In the earliest years of my ministry, I heard a message that clarified the issue in my heart. I'm not sure what biblical passage the preacher taught from, but 1 Peter 5:6 seems a likely candidate: "So humble yourselves under the mighty power of God, and at the right time he will lift you up in honor." In God's kingdom, promotion is achieved through submitting to God and drawing ever closer to him.

I began applying this principle in my own life long ago. Instead of seeking a platform, I sought the words of Scripture. Instead of seeking followers, I sought the presence of God. Instead of seeking leadership, I sought to *be led* by the Father. After a while, a wonderful thing happened—the platform ceased to matter. I was so hungry for God's Word that I simply kept pursuing avenues to learn. Even as I progressed through my PhD work, I didn't care where God would take me afterward as long as I got to serve him.

Although God has opened unbelievable doors of opportunity for me and given me multiple platforms from which to share, that still isn't the point of the story. When we submit to God, we learn that the platform isn't the point. As promised, our Father will "lift us up in honor," but we can't know when that will happen or what form it will take. In fact, honor and greatness in the eyes of God has nothing to do with our position, prominence, or platform. At the end of the day, the greatest honor we could hope to receive will be to hear "Well done, my good and faithful servant," (Matthew 25:21) when Jesus returns.

Father, thank you for helping me set priorities that lead to fulfillment and joy. Help me to desire more of your presence more than I desire position or acclaim. I repent of desiring promotion or position out of pride. Teach me to walk in humility and submission to your lordship. Give me opportunities to minister to others out of the overflow of my heart. In Jesus' name, Amen.

Personal Reflection

Write down several of your biggest dreams and goals, and prayerfully evaluate the motive behind each. Ask God if you need to shift any of your motives or reassess any of your goals. Write your thoughts below.

_____

_____

_____

_____

_____

Day 68

Day 69
Spaghetti Dinner

Growing up, Gram and Pops would often join us for family dinners. Even during my rebellious teen years, I loved those evenings and made a point to be home. One particular meal is ensconced in everyone's memory like a slow-motion car crash. Gram and Pops, as our guests, were already seated at the table. Seeking to be hospitable, I prepared Pop's plate and piled it high with steaming hot spaghetti. With the supreme grace and elegance I still possess today, I walked over and accidentally dumped the whole plate into his lap.

Let me pause to say that Pops had a quick temper. He was a kind man, but he had a short fuse and an even shorter tolerance for nonsense. The hot spaghetti in his nether region tested the furthest limits of his ability to hold his temper. So, as Pops jumped to his feet in shock and anger, everyone stood in wide-eyed paralysis. Yet, as quickly as his anger flared, Pops calmed himself with visible effort.

At that point, everyone moved into action, cleaned the mess, and we proceeded to have an enjoyable meal. I suspect that Pops, perhaps, enjoyed the meal less than the rest of us due to his wet spaghetti pants.

You may be wondering what spiritual application I could possibly derive from this story, so let me direct your attention to 1 Corinthians 8. Paul says:

> *But you must be careful so that your freedom does not cause others with a weaker conscience to stumble. . . .*

Day 69

> *And when you sin against other believers by encouraging them to do something they believe is wrong, you are sinning against Christ. So if what I eat causes another believer to sin, I will never eat meat again as long as I live—for I don't want to cause another believer to stumble.*
>
> ### 1 Corinthians 8:9, 12–13

As believers, we have the liberty to enjoy our freedom in Christ. Yet, that liberty ends where it causes another person to stumble. For example, I have the freedom to careen around the kitchen like a drunk rhino, but not if it negatively impacts my family. Because of my carelessness, I nearly induced Pops to lose his temper and sin in anger. My clumsiness serves as a simple and silly example, but the accident illustrates the importance of giving careful consideration to our actions and their potential impact.

As for a more serious example, perhaps some of your peers believe that alcohol consumption is a sin. No matter your personal belief on the issue, you should abstain in front of them so you don't entice them to sin against their own convictions. For all you know, one of your peers might struggle with alcoholism, and partaking in their presence could spark a disastrous path toward relapse.

If our Savior could give his life on our behalf, surely we can surrender a few of our own freedoms for the sake of the people he has placed in our life.

Lord, thank you for giving up your freedom and dying on the cross so that I could walk in freedom. Help me to likewise surrender my own freedoms in order to point people toward you. Teach me to be more discerning and careful in my actions, and help me be mindful of how others might perceive my behaviors. Give me self-control enough to choose a different course of action if my current plan might cause someone to stumble. In Jesus' name, Amen.

Personal Reflection

Prayerfully consider your own freedom in Christ. Might any of your hobbies, habits, or behaviors cause another person to stumble? Write down your thoughts, then ask God to help you identify at least one area in which you might need to sacrifice your own freedom to help another person grow.

_____

_____

_____

_____

_____

_____

_____

_____

_____

_____

_____

_____

Day 70
Pop's Peach Trees

Let's talk about trees, a significant theological thread in the Bible. In several winter devotionals, I provide an overview of the biblical tree theme, so let me just summarize here by saying that Jesus is the embodiment of the Tree of Life. Our Savior invites us to choose life by "eating" what he offers, and as we are nourished by him, we grow into branches bearing healthy fruit (John 15:1–8).

Pause for a moment and picture a healthy, fruitful tree—a tree with strong branches, green leaves, and ripening fruit. The images that come to my mind are my Pops' peach trees. Several of them were planted just behind the house, and Pops tended them well. Although they weren't especially large, they were lush. The dense branches literally dripped with peaches. In fact, the trees were so fruitful that we had to diligently harvest the peaches in the summer or they would fall to the ground and turn the yard into a stinky, sticky mess.

The sweet, fresh fruit was a special treat during the summer, but we continued to enjoy it long after the season ended. Gram and Pops peeled, prepped, and froze gallon bags full of peaches. I don't know what they did to that fruit, but even after being frozen, it was one of the best things I've ever tasted.

When I think about Pops' peach trees, I'm reminded of the fruit of the spirit. Paul teaches, "The Holy Spirit produces this kind of fruit in our lives: love, joy, peace, patience, kindness, goodness, faithfulness, gentleness, and self-control," (Galatians 5:22–23a). When we remain connected to our Source of life and abide in his presence, his Spirit produces wonderful fruit in our lives.

We typically focus on the personal aspect of the fruit of the Spirit, wherein we, ourselves, are transformed. Yet, the fruit of the Spirit is equally a blessing to those around us. Just as my whole family enjoyed Pops' peaches, everyone around us will benefit when we produce the fruit of the Spirit. Better still, the fruit of the Spirit will never go out of season. Our joy, patience, and kindness will bless others in good times, hard times, and everything in between. Let's bear beautiful fruit today.

Jesus, thank you for defeating death and dying on a cursed tree so that I could experience life. Fill me with your Spirit so that I can bear fruit that blesses others. Teach me to abide more fully in your presence so that I learn to better reflect your character. I ask you to endow me with a greater measure of love, joy, peace, patience, kindness, goodness, faithfulness, gentleness, and self-control. Empower me to discern the needs of others so that I bear fruit that is needed in every situation. In your name, Amen.

Personal Reflection

Memorize the fruits of the Spirit: love, joy, peace, patience, kindness, goodness, faithfulness, gentleness, and self-control. I would encourage you to write them on a notecard or type them into a digital document to carry with you. To aid the process of memory, I would also encourage you to write the verses below, perhaps even add art and color.

Day 70

Day 71
Lovely as a Tree

Yesterday we talked about the theology of trees in conjunction with the fruit of the Spirit. I would like to stay on the topic a couple more days to provide more time to consider our spiritual fruit and cultivate its growth. To become strong, fruitful trees, we must become deeply rooted in God and nourish ourselves in his presence.

This truth is illustrated well by my Gram's favorite poem, published by Joyce Kilmer in 1913. A devout Catholic, Kilmer fought and died on the front lines of World War I. Even in battle, he was renowned for his kindness, composure, and courage. I can't help but think this man understood the importance of being nourished and sustained by God's presence.

Concisely titled "Trees," Kilmer conveys a theological depth far beyond the simple attributes of trees. He writes:

I think that I shall never see
A poem lovely as a tree.
A tree whose hungry mouth is prest
Against the earth's sweet flowing breast;
A tree that looks at God all day,
And lifts her leafy arms to pray;
A tree that may in Summer wear
A nest of robins in her hair;
Upon whose bosom snow has lain;

Day 71

> *Who intimately lives with rain.*
> *Poems are made by fools like me,*
> *But only God can make a tree.*[7]

Kilmer's description of a tree provides much for us to consider. The trees hungrily seek God's nourishment; they continually look up and lift their arms in prayer; they are adorned by God's provision in seasons of warmth, and remain faithful even through seasons of rain and snow.

On the surface, Kilmer describes a tree, but his words also describe a life saturated in God's presence. Paul, immediately after he lists the fruits of the Spirit, teaches, "Those who belong to Christ Jesus have nailed the passions and desires of their sinful nature to his cross and crucified them there. Since we are living by the Spirit, let us follow the Spirit's leading in every part of our lives," (Galatians 5:24–25). When we accept the lordship of Christ, we leave our old life of sin at the cursed tree on which our Savior died. As we begin our new life through the power of the Spirit, we grow new roots, receive healthy nourishment, and begin to extend fruitful branches. This process is all encompassing and only accomplished through God's work in our heart. Just as "only God can make a tree," only he can transform us into a flourishing and fruitful bough.

Jesus, thank you for nailing my sin to the cross and giving me new life. I ask you to do a deep work in my heart and expose any roots that are still grounded in my sinful past. Teach me to abide in your presence continually and pray without ceasing. Give me the diligence to nourish myself on your Word and listen for your voice. Grow my faith so that I trust you to provide for every need, even in seasons of trial and scarcity. I pray that my life would produce an abundance of fruit that would bless the lives of others. In your name, Amen.

---

[7] *Poetry: A Magazine of Verse*, August 1913.

Personal Reflection

Review and continue memorizing the fruits of the Spirit: love, joy, peace, patience, kindness, goodness, faithfulness, gentleness, and self-control. Pray the list over yourself and ask God for a greater measure of each. As you pray, ask God to reveal one attribute he would like you to cultivate with his help today.

_____

_____

_____

_____

_____

_____

_____

_____

_____

_____

_____

_____

_____

Day 72
Bradford Pears

The last couple of days we've discussed the theology of trees and the fruit of the Spirit. We'll continue on the topic today as we talk about my least favorite type of tree: the bradford pear.

Real estate developers and home builders love bradford pear trees because they are cheap and fast-growing. The trees also lend an appealing aesthetic to new properties, especially when the trees explode into white blooms in spring. Thus, in every new subdivision, office complex, or housing development (at least in my region), builders put the finishing touch on their work with a few bradford pears. What the builders don't seem to realize is that they are planting the vegetation of Satan.

Transplanted from Asia, bradford pear trees are a blight on ecosystems throughout the midwestern and eastern regions of the US. Although the trees are planted largely in residential areas, birds transport seeds to uncultivated areas where the invasive species takes over native forests and wetlands. Even worse, the poor birds who transport the seeds prefer the sweet cyanide-laced fruit to more robust sources of nutrition, which hampers their ability to migrate successfully.

On a purely aesthetic level, the trees look appealing for a few years after they are planted. However, the branches quickly grow too large for the roots and trunk of the tree to support. Even moderate

Growth, Gardens, & Grace

storm winds can then cause a whole section of the tree to break off, leaving an asymmetrical mess that is nearly impossible to rectify.

The rancid icing on the cake is the odor produced by the trees in spring. When in bloom the trees exude a smell often compared to rotting fish. This scent in turn, attracts beetles and flies, which help pollinate and spread the invasive species. As if the smell wasn't offensive enough, the odor is symptomatic of a powerful allergen that plagues every human in proximity.

So, my point for today is that you should not plant bradford pear trees, and you should cut down any already on your property. I'm just kidding—sort of. My actual point is that we have a choice about what kind of tree we want to become. In the same chapter we've discussed the previous two days, Paul warns,

> *So I say, let the Holy Spirit guide your lives. Then you won't be doing what your sinful nature craves. The sinful nature wants to do evil, which is just the opposite of what the Spirit wants. And the Spirit gives us desires that are the opposite of what the sinful nature desires. These two forces are constantly fighting each other, so you are not free to carry out your good intentions.*

Galatians 5:16–17

Paul teaches that our old nature wars against the new life God has given us. Our sin is like a nasty bradford pear trying to invade the carefully cultivated garden of our soul. It wants to bring flies, poison fruit, rotten blossoms, and broken branches. Even worse, Paul says that our sin nature is "constantly fighting" the work of the Spirit and preventing us from carrying out our good intentions. In other words, those bradford pear trees aren't going anywhere. They will always be on my street, wafting their stink and spreading their seeds. However,

Day 72

Paul offers us a strategy for overcoming the problem. The apostle indicates that as we cultivate the fruit of the Spirit, especially in the context of community, we grow increasingly resistant to the invasive schemes of sin (Galatians 5:26–6:5). Instead of allowing the sinful shrubs to spread, our own healthy growth crowds out their advance. The sweet aroma of our spiritual fruit drowns out the stink of sin. As our roots soak up the life and love of God, the roots of rebellion begin to wither. In plain terms, practice makes perfect, or at least more like the One who is. The more we cultivate our spiritual fruit, the less opportunity sin has to take ground in our life.

Father, thank you for the gift of your Holy Spirit, who empowers me to overcome my sin nature. Equip me to protect the garden of my soul so that the Enemy cannot invade my life with his destructive schemes. Give me a greater desire to submit to you and seek you at all times. Place people in my life who will help me cultivate the fruit of the Spirit. In turn, give me opportunities to help others abide more securely in you and bear fruit in their own lives. In Jesus' name, Amen.

Personal Reflection

Review and continue memorizing the fruits of the Spirit: love, joy, peace, patience, kindness, goodness, faithfulness, gentleness, and self-control. Pray the list over yourself again and ask God for a greater measure of each. Once more, ask God to reveal one attribute he would like you to cultivate with his help today. You might work on the same one as yesterday or a different fruit the Lord places on your heart.

Growth, Gardens, & Grace

Day 73
Lake Pontchartrain

Toward the beginning of this book, I told you about some of my favorite outdoor locations in New Orleans. I would be remiss not to mention Lake Pontchartrain, which can be accessed just down the street from City Park. The winding lake shore boasts walking trails, comfortable benches, and steps right down to the water. If you plan to visit, the best time is sunset. Watching the fiery sun sink below the horizon of the calm water is truly a breathtaking experience.

Like City Park, Lake Pontchartrain is a peaceful refuge from the frenetic pace of the city. Unlike City Park, however, the cleanliness of the lake shore leaves much to be desired. Every time I've visited the area, trash litters the walking trails and steps to the water. Squashed, half-eaten food on the ground draws buzzing flies. It's a testament to the beauty of the lake that I continue to visit the area, and I'm saddened by the garbage that mars the lovely setting.

Similar to the bradford pears we discussed yesterday, when we allow our sin nature to dominate our life, we allow the Enemy to throw garbage all over the beautiful garden God is cultivating in our souls. Instead of bearing the fruit of the spirit, we get rotten leftovers ground into the dirt and covered in flies. Paul describes these anti-fruits of the Spirit: "When you follow the desires of your sinful nature, the results are very clear: sexual immorality, impurity, lustful pleasures, idolatry, sorcery, hostility, quarreling, jealousy, outbursts of anger, selfish ambition, dissension, division, envy, drunkenness, wild parties, and other sins like these," (Galatians 5:19–21a). Lest we skim over the list because we think that we wouldn't be tempted to commit the so-called "big sins," let's be sure to read each item. I'll bet we've all struggled at some point with anger, jealousy, selfishness, envy, and even some additional sins that aren't on Paul's list.

Although the Enemy wages a constant battle to sully our souls, he has already been defeated by Christ at the Cross. Jesus wiped our sins away and cleansed our souls, and through his gift of the Holy Spirit, we are equipped to resist the dirty schemes of the Enemy.

Many years ago the state of Texas began an anti-littering campaign with the slogan: "Don't mess with Texas." Ironically, I "decorated" the walls of Gram and Pops' house with stickers bearing the slogan and created a huge mess. Instead of making a mess or allowing the Enemy to litter the landscape of our souls, let's stand up to him and boldly declare that he is a loser, a liar, and he can't "mess with" our souls.

Jesus, thank you for washing away my sin and turning the littered landscape of my soul into a beautiful haven. Holy Spirit, thank you for equipping me and empowering me to resist the schemes of the Enemy and the temptations of my flesh. Grow my faith, perseverance, and self-control so that I'm able to better guard my heart. Produce in me an abundant yield of the fruit of the Spirit. Make my soul so peaceful and pure that others see you through my life. In your name, Amen.

Personal Reflection

Review and continue memorizing the fruits of the Spirit: love, joy, peace, patience, kindness, goodness, faithfulness, gentleness, and self-control. Pray the list over yourself again and ask God for a greater measure of each. In addition, survey the landscape of your soul and

Day 73

look for any sin that might be dirtying the beautiful terrain God has cultivated in you. Ask God to show you how you can replace that rotten fruit of sin with the healthy fruit of the Holy Spirit.

Day 74
Melissa — *Part 1*

Since we've been discussing the fruit of the Spirit over the last few days, I would like to tell you about someone in my life who positively exudes them. My friend Melissa, despite every reason to be a bitter and angry person, is one of the most loving, patient, and kind people I know. She is one of those people who simply puts you at ease. You can't help but feel peaceful in her gentle presence. You would never know that deep, gut-wrenching trauma lies in her past.

I first met Melissa when she moved to our city and began attending our church. I soon learned that she had moved from California to Alabama—literally across the entire country—to flee from an abusive husband. With three children under the age of 5, Melissa was starting a new life as a single mom. I was impressed by her bravery, but not surprised by the situation. Sadly, domestic violence is not uncommon, and I'd counseled numerous women in similar situations—or so I thought.

After many years of pastoral ministry, I'm not surprised by much of anything. While I have great love and compassion for the people to whom I minister, I've learned to protect my heart and maintain my emotional equilibrium. Yet, the evening Melissa shared her story with me, I went home and cried into my pillow.

Melissa's ex-husband had surpassed what we would refer to as domestic violence. In fact, he was in prison for human torture. I won't go into detail except to say that Melissa's hair, which I thought

Day 74

was simply cut into a cute bob, was actually growing out because her head had been forcibly shaved.

Although her ex-husband had been charged and incarcerated with relative expediency, Melissa knew he would eventually be released on parole—thus the move to Alabama. Shockingly, one of her first steps was to find a church. Although her ex-husband had often claimed that his punishments were on God's behalf, Melissa knew otherwise. She clung to her Father and sustained her faith through Scripture. Through her years of abuse and subsequent escape, she took courage from Psalm 23:

The Lord is my shepherd;
I have all that I need.
He lets me rest in green meadows;
he leads me beside peaceful streams.
He renews my strength.
He guides me along right paths,
bringing honor to his name.
Even when I walk through the darkest valley,
I will not be afraid, for you are close beside me.
Your rod and your staff protect and comfort me.
You prepare a feast for me in the presence of my
enemies.
You honor me by anointing my head with oil.
My cup overflows with blessings.
Surely your goodness and unfailing love will pursue
me all the days of my life,
and I will live in the house of the Lord forever.
Psalm 23

In Melissa's own words, "I knew that the Lord was with me even in the darkest moments when I wondered if I was going to survive."

In my own moments of struggle and strife, which pale in comparison by far, Melissa's example of faith and resilience inspires me. I pray it inspires you as well.

Lord, thank you for protecting my life and providing everything I need. Thank you for renewing my strength and refreshing my soul. Forgive me for doubting your goodness. Teach me to follow you along the paths in which you lead me. Help me to trust that you are by my side even when I walk down pathways that are difficult. Enable me to see the blessings you've given me even on my darkest days. Empower me to be an example of strength, faith, and resilience so that I can lead others to your love. In Jesus' name, Amen.

Personal Reflection

Re-read Psalm 23 and write down what each line means to you. For example: "He lets me rest in green meadows" = God refreshes my soul when I ride my bike, float in the lake, and hike with my family. You can write in the margins beside the Scripture or use the lines below.

_____

_____

_____

_____

_____

Day 74

Day 75
Melissa — Part 2

Today, I would like to give you a bit more of Melissa's story. Although we won't go into great detail, the events may be difficult to read. If you are a sensitive soul, you may want to skip the next three paragraphs.

On the day the police were called to her home, the situation was dire. Melissa knew she was about to be killed because her husband had gone outside to get a tarp for her soon-to-be-dead body. Calling for help was almost as frightening as allowing herself to be murdered because her abuser had also threatened her whole family. He had warned her that if she ever sought help or tried to leave, he would kill her parents, her brothers, and their children. Chillingly, he had even provided details on how he would do it.

Yet, on that day Melissa fully surrendered to her Heavenly Father. She already had faith, but it wasn't until that day that she began to trust God without reservation. She trusted him with all the unknowns of her future and with the safety of her family. In her words, "I knew I had to surrender myself fully to the Lord and trust him with my life, literally. I knew he wouldn't let me fall." As she moved forward in faith, she claimed the words of Psalm 46:5: "God is within her, she will not fall; God will help her as the morning dawns," (my translation).

Therefore, when her husband walked outside for the tarp, she called her mom for help, who immediately called the police. Yet, when the officers arrived, Melissa faced another challenge to her new-found courage. You see, officers aren't allowed to intervene in a domestic

Day 75

dispute unless one party requests aid. Therefore, Melissa had to indict her husband of his abuse. So, fearing reprisal, yet clinging to her faith, she asked the officers for help. Her husband was immediately taken into custody and imprisoned thereafter.

At that moment, Melissa ceased to be a victim. Melissa realized that her Savior had already broken every chain that bound her, but she was responsible to leave her chains behind. She was a victim only as long as she continued to believe she was a victim. Instead of rooting her identity in oppression, she accepted God's truth that she was, and is, an overcomer.

Today, Melissa is thriving in her personal, professional, and spiritual life. Her three children are the most adorable and joyful kids you can imagine. She testifies to his faithfulness: "It shows you how much God can change things when you truly lay your life in his hands."

Father, thank you for your steadfast love and protection. Help me to trust you not just with parts of my life, but with my whole life. Enable me to see myself in the light of your love. Expose the lies I believe about myself and empower me to claim my identity as a beloved child of God. Teach me to see myself as a victor rather than a victim. Teach me to walk in the power of the Holy Spirit and the confidence of my faith. In Jesus' name, Amen.

Personal Reflection

Past trauma can impact our life in one of two ways. We will either overcome, learn, and grow from our experiences or we will remain in a state of perpetual victimhood and arrested development. Consider any major traumas or trials in your past. How have they shaped the person you have become? Prayerfully reflect and write your thoughts below.[8]

---

[8] If you are healing from trauma, consider reaching out to a pastor and/or professional counselor.

Growth, Gardens, & Grace

Day 76
Bread of Life

When I became a Christ follower, fasting was mysterious and confusing to me. I never heard a sermon on the topic, and no one in my spiritual circle discussed fasting outright. After repeatedly encountering biblical passages about fasting, however, I finally mustered the courage to ask a spiritual mentor about it. Was fasting something that believers actually do? How could refusing to eat help me grow spiritually? Was I sinning against God by *not* fasting?

Today, fasting is a much more common topic, both in the church and in the secular world. Advances in nutritional science have proven the physiological benefits of fasting and the physical fitness community has adopted the practice wholeheartedly. However, the physical impact is only a peripheral benefit of a true spiritual fast.[9]

As we've discussed the last few days, two natures are at war within us: our carnal desire to sin and our spiritual desire to live for God. Just as cultivating the fruit of the Spirit helps us overcome our desire to disobey God, fasting likewise trains us to overcome our base impulses. As we refrain from eating, we develop greater self-discipline and build the spiritual muscles to deny other fleshly impulses. As we deprive our bodies, we simultaneously feed our spirit, which grows stronger and more deeply rooted in the Lord.

---

[9] If you'd like to learn more about fasting, I recommend *Fasting: The Ancient Practices* by Scot McKnight (Thomas Nelson, 2010).

Allow me to illustrate with succulents. A hardy, desert plant, succulents don't require an abundance of water. Most of them are easy to propagate because any bit of stem or leaf that falls from the parent plant can grow its own roots. As the new plant seeks to become rooted, it grows best in the absence of water. Because the offshoot is no longer receiving nutrients from its parent, the baby succulent sends roots into the soil. In other words, the plant's desire for sustenance causes it to become more deeply rooted.

When we fast, we experience an acute need for sustenance. By refusing to meet that need with food or other physical comforts, our spirit sends out hungry tendrils that become more deeply rooted in the Lord. As God nourishes our souls, we increasingly realize that the desires of the flesh are a poor substitute for a closer walk with our Savior. Jesus said to the crowds that followed him, "The true bread of God is the one who comes down from heaven and gives life to the world … I am the bread of life. Whoever comes to me will never be hungry again. Whoever believes in me will never be thirsty," (John 6:33, 35). Eating food keeps our bodies alive, but only the love of God gives us *life*.

Jesus, thank you for nourishing my soul and giving me an abundant life. Help me to step beyond my comfort zone and seek you more diligently than ever before. Give me a hunger for your Word and your presence that is greater than any fleshly desire. Give me the strength and self-discipline to feed my spirit through regular fasting, prayer and study. In your name, Amen.

Personal Reflection

Consider observing a fast the future. If the practice is new to you, start out by simply skipping one meal and replacing it with prayer and Bible study. If you have experience with fasting, you may want to plan for a whole day soon. If you are considering a fast longer than one day, I recommend talking to a spiritual mentor and a physician first.

Day 76

Day 77
Fast Facts

Yesterday we discussed the spiritual discipline of fasting. Because the practice is so often misunderstood, I would like to spend one more day on the topic. A fast, technically, can be abstaining from just about anything. We can fast from social media, television, video games, or shopping. We can even abstain from food, yet not experience any spiritual growth or benefit. So, what is the type of fast that is described in Scripture? To answer that question, I'd like to give you four "fast facts" about fasting. (Get it?)

First, a true biblical fast involves abstaining from food or drink for a period of time to draw nearer to God. As you fast, remember that fasting is turning to God, becoming more surrendered to him, and listening for his voice. When we refrain from preparing and eating food, we save time that we can devote to spending with God. On a deeper level, fasting builds our spiritual strength and self-control to overcome sinful desires. As our spirit grows stronger and our hearts more pure, we can then hear the voice of the Lord more clearly. In short, if our primary focus is skipping meals, we've missed the point.

Second, men and women throughout Scripture model the practice of fasting prior to important decisions. Since fasting empowers us to more clearly hear God's voice, observing a fast can help us discern his will and continue walking in his plan for our life. I'm sure we've all made a few bad decisions we wish we could do over!

Day 77

Similarly, biblical fasts are often observed in response to a need. Although we can't bribe or coerce God by fasting, he does respond to the devotion of his children, often moving in supernatural ways. In situations where God does not meet the "need" for which we pray, our fast often draws us close enough to his heart to see a better path forward.

Third, fasting equips us to become better ministers of the Gospel because it sets us apart from the world. Our culture encourages us to satisfy every desire and indulge in every pleasure. By living with purity and self-control, we show the world a path of health and wholeness that brings true joy. When Daniel fasted from rich food, meat, wine, and even lotion, the Persians thought he was crazy, but as he grew healthier and wiser, he gained favor in their eyes. Daniel's fast allowed the Persians to see that he served a powerful God!

Fasting, if done correctly, reminds me to take the focus off of me. Isaiah sums up the situation well:

> *This is the kind of fasting I want:*
> *Free those who are wrongly imprisoned;*
> *lighten the burden of those who work for you.*
> *Let the oppressed go free,*
> *and remove the chains that bind people.*
> *Share your food with the hungry,*
> *and give shelter to the homeless.*
> *Give clothes to those who need them,*
> *and do not hide from relatives who need your help.*
> *Then your salvation will come like the dawn,*
> *and your wounds will quickly heal.*
> *Your godliness will lead you forward,*
> *and the glory of the Lord will protect you from behind.*

Then when you call, the Lord will answer.
'Yes, I am here,' he will quickly reply.
Isaiah 58:6–9

When we fast, we become more like Jesus. As he pours his love into our hearts, it overflows onto others. In doing so, our own wounds are healed and our needs are filled.

Father, thank you for teaching me practical steps through which I can draw nearer to you. Show me how I can make fasting a regular part of my spiritual health and growth. Give me a greater measure of self-control and help me be diligent to deny my sinful impulses. Help me live in such a way that others see that true contentment comes from you rather than indulging every desire. As I fast, I pray you would open doors of opportunity for me to help people who need your message of freedom and salvation. In Jesus' name, Amen.

Personal Reflection

Yesterday, I encouraged you to plan for a time to fast in the near future. If you haven't yet chosen a date, do so now and write it below. Then make a list of any upcoming decisions or needs about which you would like to pray during your fast. When the time/day of your fast arrives, remember to revisit your list.

_____

_____

_____

_____

Day 77

Day 78
Jonah

I must confess, I have a strong aversion to the prophet Jonah. I feel a little guilty because I believe we should respect the men and women of God whose ministries are recorded in Scripture. My problem is that I have trouble regarding Jonah as a man of God. In my mind, he is more of a sullen brat. Allow me to explain.

As soon as the Lord called Jonah to the city of Nineveh, the prophet fled. Jonah ran from God by chartering a boat, and his presence endangered the life of every ship-mate. Once he was thrown overboard, the prophet was famously swallowed by a "giant fish" (Jonah 1:17). Fearing for his life, Jonah prayed an eloquent prayer from the belly of his whale.

I can't help but snicker when I read the grandiose words of Jonah, which starkly contrast the statement that immediately follows: "Then the Lord spoke to the fish, and it vomited Jonah onto the dry land," (Jonah 2:10, my translation). Thus, cowed and humbled, Jonah obediently traveled to Nineveh, the capital city of the Assyrian empire.

An enemy of Israel, the Assyrians were brutal conquerors. So, when the Ninevites heeded Jonah's message of repentance and received the forgiveness of God, the prophet "became exceedingly displeased, and was angry," (Jonah 4:1, my translation). Despite the beautiful and repentant-sounding words Jonah had prayed, his heart was still set against the will of the Father. Jonah was so bitter, in fact,

Day 78

that he walked out of the city, sat down under a tree, and wished for death. The end! Can you see why I struggle with Jonah?

Recently, however, God helped me see the book and the prophet in a new light. As I read, my Father asked, "Is your problem with Jonah or yourself?" And I realized that all the qualities that bother me about Jonah are flaws I see in myself. Ouch! I can pray beautiful prayers and deliver powerful messages then catch myself rebelling against God's guidance a short time later. Sometimes when I don't get my way, I become sullen and angry. In extreme cases, I'll even sit and pout under my metaphorical tree, wishing for God to strike me dead.

As I've grown older and more mature, my rebellious, dramatic, and overly emotional tendencies have diminished under the tutelage of the Holy Spirit. However, my shortcomings are still with me, always waiting for an opportunity to rise up.

I've discovered that self-awareness is key. Instead of judging rashly, I can respond thoughtfully. Instead of scorning the flaws of others, I can examine my own heart. So, the next time someone gets under our skin, let's pause, reflect, and ask what we can learn about ourselves.

Father, thank you for the example of Jonah, who shows me the grief and hopelessness of a life lived in rebellion against you. Help me learn from his example and walk in faith and obedience. I ask you to uproot any rebellion, selfishness, or hate in my heart. Through your Spirit, allow me to recognize my own shortcomings so that I can take steps to overcome them. When I notice traits about other people that bother me, help me to examine myself rather than judging them. Teach me to trust you even when you lead me to paths upon which I don't want to walk. Align my heart with yours so that following you is my greatest desire. In Jesus' name, Amen.

Personal Reflection

Today, as you notice behaviors or traits that bother you in other people, ask God to show you what you can learn about yourself.

Day 79
Nahum & Nineveh

Yesterday we discussed my change of heart toward the rebellious prophet Jonah. Part of the process was my reading of Nahum, a prophetic oracle against Nineveh, the city to which God called Jonah and the capital city of Assyria.

At the height of their power during the period of Jonah and Nahum, the Assyrian forces were brutal in their conquest of the region. The aggressive empire began attacking Israel and exacting tributes around 850 BC and continued to do so until 721 BC, when they destroyed Jerusalem and deported her people.

I'm well aware of these historical details, which likely form the backdrop of Jonah's resistance to minister to Nineveh. Yet, when I recently read Nahum's oracle, I felt a new sympathy for Jonah. Nahum prophesied,

> *What sorrow awaits Nineveh, the city of murder and lies!*
> *She is crammed with wealth, and is never without victims.*
> *Hear the crack of whips, the rumble of wheels!*
> *Horses' hooves pound, and chariots clatter wildly.*
> *See the flashing swords and glittering spears as the charioteers charge past!*
> *There are countless casualties, heaps of bodies—*

so many bodies that people stumble over them.
All this because Nineveh, the beautiful and faithless city,
mistress of deadly charms, enticed the nations with her beauty.
She taught them all her magic, enchanting people everywhere.

. . .

All who hear of your destruction will clap their hands for joy.
Where can anyone be found who has not suffered from your continual cruelty?
Nahum (3:1–4, 19)

If Nahum's accusations seem harsh, they are corroborated by the historical documents of the Assyrians themselves, who boast of their macabre brutalities. In such a light, I can more easily empathize with Jonah's recalcitrance.

The point I'm trying to make is that we often make snap judgments based on incomplete knowledge and insufficient understanding. My judgment of Jonah was unfair and inaccurate because I haven't lived under the threat of Assyrian oppression. In colloquial terms, I haven't "walked in his shoes." So, if God has compassion enough for a man like Jonah and a city like Nineveh, I should strive to follow his example of grace and forgiveness.

All people, whether sinners or saints, deserve compassion. According to Hebrews 13:3, "Remember those in prison, as if you were there yourself. Remember also those being mistreated, as if you felt their pain in your own bodies." Showing compassion, grace, and love doesn't mean that we condone hurtful actions, sins, or crimes, but it

Day 79

does mean that we acknowledge each person's God-given value as a human. From the saint in church to the murderer in prison, each bears the image of God. We may never know what led each person to where they are, but we know that they are loved by our Father. Let's look through his eyes today.

Father, thank you for being a God of both love and justice. I'm grateful that I can trust you to judge capably and wisely. Help me be quick to extend empathy and compassion rather than judgment and disdain. Teach me to speak words seasoned with grace instead of anger or hate. Empower me to see all of your children through your eyes and minister to them as you lead me. In Jesus' name, Amen.

Personal Reflection

Yesterday, you gave special attention to behaviors or traits that bother you in other people and asked God to show you what you can learn about yourself. Continue to do so today, but also be proactive about offering kindness, empathy, and compassion in each instance.

_____

_____

_____

_____

_____

_____

_____

Growth, Gardens, & Grace

Day 80
Shrewd as Snakes

Yesterday we talked about showing compassion and leaving judgment in God's hands. Today, I would like to clarify the difference between judging and evaluating. Although Jesus commands us not to judge others (Matthew 7:1), he also calls us to use discernment. In Matthew 10:16, Jesus says, "Look, I am sending you out as sheep among wolves. So be as shrewd as snakes and harmless as doves." You and I are like dumb, docile sheep in the midst of cunning, vicious predators.

Jesus' teaching may be more apt than we realize. Although snakes aren't especially intelligent, they have gifts that enable them to survive and thrive. The tongue, in particular, gives snakes an advantage in evaluating the world around them. With each flick, a snake gathers microscopic particles from the air, which are then transferred into the mouth and passed onto the brain for analysis. The fork in the tongue even helps the snake determine from which direction each scent originates.

Equipped with information about the surrounding environment, a snake can then determine the best course of action. Should it eat a nearby meal? Should it flee so that it doesn't become a meal? Should it pursue a potential mate?

Like snakes, we might not always be smart enough to outwit our Enemy, but our Father endows us with the faculties to overcome his schemes. Primary among our gifts are faith and wisdom. Through faithful adherence to the wise principles God provides in

Scripture, we can evaluate every situation and determine a prudent course of action.

Our spiritual discernment is a bit like the snake's tongue, with which we test the atmosphere around us. For example, I can refuse to judge a fellow human and value their worth as a child of God. Yet, if I evaluate our interaction and determine that the person has an intent to harm me, I will end our exchange and retreat to safety. Similarly, if I discern that a particular friend indulges in unhealthy habits that detrimentally impact my own physical and spiritual health, I should use my God-given discernment to help my friend find freedom or find healthier friends.

In short, we don't have to be the sharpest tool in the shed as long as we allow ourselves to be wielded by the hand of our Father.

Father, thank you for providing me with wisdom and discernment. Make me more sensitive to the guidance of the Holy Spirit, and teach me to hear your voice more clearly. Forgive me for ignoring your direction and going my own way. Increase my capacity for making wise choices, and give me a greater desire to walk in obedience. Help me withhold judgment and love all people while also making healthy decisions about how I should respond to each individual and situation. In Jesus' name, Amen.

Personal Reflection

Today, practice evaluating people and situations without judging. Make an effort to mentally (maybe even verbally) affirm people with whom you interact, yet also evaluate how each interaction and individual impacts your health and growth. As you use your faculty of discernment, be sure to move in every direction the Spirit leads you.

Day 80

Day 81
Country Bumpkin

Since we talked about Jonah and Nahum a couple of days ago, I thought I would tell you about the prophet Amos today. Even among the diverse personalities and ministries of the biblical prophets, Amos stands out.

Roughly 50–75 years before Israel fell to Assyria, Amos warned the people of God's impending judgment. At this time in history, the Jewish people were divided into two nations: Israel and Judah. Although Amos lived in Judea, God called him to prophecy in Israel. Even more surprising, Amos was a humble shepherd. The unassuming prophet went so far as to call himself a *boles*, which is literally translated "fig-slitter," but figuratively refers to a "country bumpkin" or "unsophisticated farmer" (Amos 7:14).[10] Nonetheless, when God called Amos, the prophet didn't resist like Moses or flee like Jonah. He simply walked away from his farm and obeyed the Lord.

As Amos delivered God's call to repentance, his message garnered such attention that his words reached the ears of the king. In today's terms Amos' prophecies went viral. Unfortunately, the people's response to Amos was not a positive one. Jeroboam, the king, and Amaziah, the priest, told Amos to go back to his farm. Or in my liberal paraphrase of Amos 7:12, they said, "Get out of here, you

---

[10] James Swanson, "*balas*," *Dictionary of Biblical Languages with Semantic Domains: Hebrew* (Oak Harbor: Logos, 1997).

Day 81

hillbilly. Go back where you came from and stop bothering us. You aren't even worthy to eat bread in the king's city." Yet, Amos, standing before the most powerful men in the country, wasn't cowed. He boldly responded:

> *You say, "Don't prophesy against Israel.*
> *Stop preaching against my people."*
> *But this is what the Lord says:*
> *"Your wife will become a prostitute in this city,*
> *and your sons and daughters will be killed.*
> *Your land will be divided up,*
> *and you yourself will die in a foreign land.*
> *And the people of Israel will certainly become captives in exile,*
> *far from their homeland."*
>
> **Amos 7:16b–17**

Amos had guts! Nothing could deter him from standing firm in his faith and declaring God's truth.

What can we learn from Amos? First, when God calls, we can respond with confidence. The only qualification required is faith—not heritage, nor education, nor race, nor status. As we walk with our Father, he equips us with every skill we need. Second, our success is measured by obedience, not outcome. Amos could have considered his ministry a failure when he was rejected and ridiculed. Yet, instead of listening to the criticism of men, he continued listening to the voice of God.

So, to whose voice will we listen today? Will we listen to our own inner critic, who says that we aren't smart enough or eloquent enough to speak about our faith? Will we listen to the Enemy when he says we aren't good enough or righteous enough to share the Good News? Will we fear what others might say if we walk in bold obedience? Let's shut down the trash talk and tune into the only voice that matters—that of our Father.

Father, thank you for declaring me worthy to share your message of repentance, love, and grace. Teach me to discern your voice among the many other voices I hear daily. Help me listen only to you as I tune out the lies of the Enemy. I repent of remaining silent out of fear of what others might think or say. Empower me to walk with confidence and obedience so that I can accomplish your perfect will in my life and world. In Jesus' name, Amen.

Personal Reflection

Prayerfully reflect on your attitude toward sharing your faith or taking bold steps of obedience. Do you feel intimidated or nervous? Do you feel like you aren't good enough or don't have enough biblical knowledge? Are you worried you might get a question you can't answer? (It's ok to say "I don't know.") Are you worried about what others might think of you? Make a list of your thoughts, fears, and doubts below. Then, go back through your list and write a faith-filled statement of the truth to replace each doubt and fear.

_____

_____

_____

_____

_____

_____

_____

_____

Day 81

Day 82
Got Talents?

Yesterday, we discussed walking in confident obedience per the example of Amos, who boldly shared the message of the Lord. As children of God, we've been given the extravagant gift of redemption, and like Amos, we are called to share that gift. In fact, our very existence should reflect the nature of God's Kingdom as we invite others to become a part. To illustrate, let's reflect on the words of Jesus himself. In the passage that is often referred to as "The Parable of the Talents," our Lord says,

> *The Kingdom of Heaven can be illustrated by the story of a man going on a long trip. He called together his servants and entrusted his money to them while he was gone. He gave five bags of silver to one, two bags of silver to another, and one bag of silver to the last—dividing it in proportion to their abilities. He then left on his trip. . . . After a long time their master returned from his trip and called them to give an account of how they had used his money. The servant to whom he had entrusted the five bags of silver came forward with five more and said, "Master, you gave me five bags of silver to invest, and I have earned five more." The master was full of praise. "Well done, my good*

Day 82

and faithful servant. You have been faithful in handling this small amount, so now I will give you many more responsibilities. Let's celebrate together!" . . . Then the servant with the one bag of silver came and said, "Master, I knew you were a harsh man, harvesting crops you didn't plant and gathering crops you didn't cultivate. I was afraid I would lose your money, so I hid it in the earth. Look, here is your money back." But the master replied, "You wicked and lazy servant!"

Matthew 25:14–15, 19–21, 24–26a

The "good and faithful servant" utilized the gifts he had been given. He invested his resources on behalf of his master. He didn't let fear of failure prevent him from making bold choices and taking calculated risks, unlike the "wicked and lazy servant."

Sometimes, our fear of stepping out or speaking up arises because we haven't invested wisely. Perhaps God is calling us to hone a talent we've ignored, learn a skill we've neglected, or relinquish a bad habit. Perhaps he is leading us to take a Bible study or enroll in a course to learn more about Scripture. Perhaps he is calling us to create a budget and manage our financial resources more wisely. Only you know what steps God is calling you to take.

Let me be clear that our Lord loves us lavishly and unconditionally. However, each of us will one day stand before him and answer for how we have utilized our time, resources, and talents. How does your investment portfolio look?

Father, thank you for providing all the resources I need to grow in faith and serve you well. Teach me to hone my talents and utilize them for your glory. Guide me to a deeper knowledge of your Word and your character. Give me the self-control to manage my financial resources wisely and overcome harmful habits. Open my eyes to opportunities to invest in your Kingdom by serving others and sharing your love. In Jesus' name, Amen.

Personal Reflection

Review your notes from yesterday. Brainstorm and make a new list of practical steps you can take to alleviate your fears and build your confidence. After your list is complete, prayerfully choose one step you can take to invest in your faith. If you aren't sure where to start, ask a spiritual mentor for suggestions.

_____

_____

_____

_____

_____

_____

_____

_____

_____

_____

Day 83
Fun in the Sun

Spring is the most fun season of the year for me. As the weather warms, I rejoice that I've survived another cold winter—dramatic, I know—and abandon my work to play outside. I hike, bike, dig in the garden, swim in the lake, and anything else that involves being outdoors. The fun of moving my body in the warm sunshine refreshes my soul like nothing else.

Did you know that fun is a biblical concept? God isn't like a grouchy old man yelling at kids to get off his lawn. Our Father created the concept of fun and planted a need for it in our hearts. Fun rejuvenates our souls and provides a break from the daily grind of life. It refills our joy tank, which sustains us through tedious and difficult seasons of life. Although God calls us to work hard, through joyful moments he gives us the endurance and strength to do so.

The author of Ecclesiastes heartily endorses having fun and enjoying life. He encourages, "I recommend having fun, because there is nothing better for people in this world than to eat, drink, and enjoy life. That way they will experience some happiness along with all the hard work God gives them under the sun," (Ecclesiastes 8:15).

The divine directive to have fun isn't a license to overindulge or transgress God's commands. Instead, true enjoyment of life takes place within the freedom that obedience provides—freedom from addiction, lust, heartache, and bankruptcy. In teaching us to truly enjoy life, our Father protects us from excesses that can destroy us. When we listen to God and have fun his way, we'll wake up the next morning with a refreshed soul rather than a hangover!

Father, thank you for offering a myriad of blessings for me to enjoy in this life. Equip me to work hard while also enjoying the fruit of my labor. Give me the discipline to refrain from pastimes that deplete my body and soul. Show me how I can incorporate healthy fun into my rhythm of life. In Jesus' name, Amen.

Personal Reflection

What pastimes and recreational activities are fun for you? Make a list below and then choose one to enjoy this week!

_____

_____

_____

_____

_____

_____

_____

_____

_____

_____

Day 83

Day 84
Divine Deconstruction

My younger son, Abel, routinely takes things apart to see how they work. As soon as he could walk and talk, Abel began experimenting to see how the world works. Even now, we routinely find remnants of unusual experiments and bizarre creations around the house, which we've simply labeled "science" since other words fail to describe Abel's handiwork. At one point, he had two old televisions and a broken ceiling fan in his bedroom. The mess drives me crazy, but I love that he loves to learn.

I understand Abel's drive to learn and experiment because I feel the same way. I recall once, as a child, unscrewing the faceplate of an electrical outlet and jabbing the wiring with a screwdriver. I knew I wasn't supposed to stick anything into an outlet, but I wanted to see what would happen if I did. Fortunately, I only received a little shock, and it was strong enough to dissuade me from further investigation.

Even after many years of schooling, I still feel the same drive to learn. In my younger years, I satisfied my scientific curiosity with a degree in chemical engineering. Now, my primary subject of study is God and his Word. As I've continued to gain knowledge, I've realized just how much I still have to learn, not only about God, but about his entire creation. Our Father is so far beyond us, that we will never fully understand who he is or how he works in the world, at least not in this lifetime (Isaiah 55:8–9).

Day 84

The author of Ecclesiastes describes the inscrutable nature of God and his work in the world: "In my search for wisdom and in my observation of people's burdens here on earth, I discovered that there is ceaseless activity, day and night. I realized that no one can discover everything God is doing under the sun. Not even the wisest people discover everything, no matter what they claim," (Ecclesiastes 8:16–17). No matter how hard we work, strive, study, or experiment, we simply don't have the capacity to fully understand God and his ways. Although our lack of knowledge makes us feel vulnerable, we can have peace because our infinitely powerful Father is fully in control.

I'm glad I serve a God who is smarter and more powerful than me. I'm fine with not understanding every detail about the universe because I don't have to run it. I'm okay with not understanding everything about my Father because that means he is more intelligent than me.

Although we should always strive to learn more about God and his ways, we must also learn to be content when we reach the limits of our understanding. Where knowledge stops, faith grows. We know our God is good and we know he loves us, so we can trust him with the things we don't know.

Father, I praise you for your unsurpassed power and limitless knowledge. Forgive me for becoming angry with you or doubting your goodness simply because I don't understand how you are working in the world. I ask you to teach me more about you, your character, your Word, and your plans, yet help me trust you even when I don't understand. In Jesus' name, Amen.

Personal Reflection

Prayerfully reflect and write down a few areas of life and faith in which you would like God to give you greater understanding. Perhaps you would like to know why God allowed a tragedy or difficult situation to take place. Perhaps you would like to understand how your faith is compatible with science. Perhaps you would like to learn your purpose in life or the meaning of the universe. Ask your Father to reveal greater insight and helpful resources. At the same time, ask him to help you become more comfortable with the discomfort of not fully understanding.

_____

_____

_____

_____

_____

_____

_____

_____

_____

_____

_____

Day 84

Day 85
Mother's Day

Since we are in proximity to Mother's Day, I would like to tell you about a unique animal mom—more specifically, a reptile mom. Female alligators are among the best mothers in the natural world, which I find delightful considering their ferocity and power.

Alligator moms start preparing for their babies by building a comfy nest. They gather sticks, reeds, and other plant matter upon which they will lay 30–50 eggs. They then cover the eggs with more vegetation to hide them from predators. During the subsequent 70(ish) days of incubation, the mother alligator never strays far from her eggs. Finally, when the babies are ready to hatch, they cry out from inside the eggs, and their attentive mother helps extricate them from their shells.

Although alligators were once thought to eat their young like many other species of reptile, the mother actually carries them in her mouth. With her massive jaws and sharp teeth, mama alligator carefully and gently carries each of her young to the water. And with 30–50 babies, I'm sure that takes a while! Once in the water, mom protects her young for up to a year, at which point they are large enough to feed and care for themselves.

Like the female alligator, human moms are also fierce. To care for our children well, we must cultivate resilience, fortitude, and tenacity along with empathy, patience, and kindness. In Proverbs 31, King Lemuel lauds the virtues of mothers and wives:

Day 85

> *An excellent wife who can find?*
> *She is far more precious than jewels.*
> *The heart of her husband trusts in her, and he will have no lack of gain.*
> *She does him good, and not harm, all the days of her life.*
> *She finds wool and flax and busily spins it.*
> *She is like a merchant's ship, bringing her food from afar.*
> *She gets up before dawn to prepare breakfast for her household*
> *and plan the day's work for her servant girls.*
>
> . . .
>
> *She looks well to the ways of her household*
> *and does not eat the bread of idleness.*
> *Her children rise up and call her blessed;*
> *her husband also, and he praises her:*
> *"Many women have done excellently, but you surpass them all."*
> *Charm is deceitful, and beauty is vain,*
> *but a woman who fears the LORD is to be praised.*
>
> **Proverbs 31:10-15, 27-30**

As wives and mothers, God calls us to be diligent in following him and tenacious in caring for our families. We must be gentle enough to carry our babies in our arms but strong enough to fight off attacks against them.

Sadly, the roles of a wife and mother have increasingly been devalued in our culture. Instead of being desired, the role of motherhood has come to be viewed as a distraction from personal goals. Rather than being lauded for her familial devotion, the stay-at-home mom is regarded as someone who has "given up" the chance for a "real" career. In God's eyes, however, the roles of wife and mother are praiseworthy beyond compare!

I want to emphasize that whether you go to work, stay home, work from home, or anything else, your role as a wife and/or mom is valuable. Your husband and children aren't a distraction, they are your first and foremost calling. If you are a mom, celebrate the amazing opportunities God has given you to minister to your family. If you aren't a mom, be sure to celebrate those who are!

Father, thank you for the mothers who have poured their love and wisdom into my life. I pray you would bless them today. Teach me to appreciate the various roles to which you have called me, and equip me to fulfill them wisely. Forgive me for comparing myself to other people and being dissatisfied with my own life. Help me walk with healthy reverence toward you and your calling on my life. Guide me as I seek to tend to the beauty of my soul so that I can effectively care for the people with whom you have entrusted me. In Jesus' name, Amen.

Personal Reflection

Reach out to a mother, mother-figure, or female mentor who has impacted your life and thank her today.

_____

_____

_____

_____

Day 85

Day 86
Chocolate Mimosa

My home is surrounded by a variety of trees. From the massive river birch to the small eucalyptus, each is lovely and unique. One tree is especially distinctive—my chocolate mimosa. In the spring, the branches sprout fluffy pink blooms and delicate purple leaves.

I was therefore broken-hearted when the tree became infested with tent worms. In case you aren't familiar, the pests weave thick webs in the branches of trees and feed on the leaves. Although they can live in a tree for years before killing it, the foliage begins to look repulsive, covered in webs, worms, and dead leaves. Even worse, the notoriously hard to kill worms will spread to surrounding trees.

I recall, as a child, watching Pops go to war against the parasites when they invaded his beloved pecan trees. In my memory, he spent weeks climbing up and down his ladder to prune infested branches and burn wormy nests. I don't know if the process actually took as long as I recall, but I wasn't willing to risk a complete infestation in my yard. So, with a heavy heart, I chopped down my beautiful mimosa.

You can, therefore, imagine my joy when a new tree sprouted the following spring. From the base of the severed trunk, a new mimosa began to grow. It has continued to grow over the years and even surpassed the size of the original tree! In the spring, we enjoy the pink flowers— my niece especially loves to pick the blossoms and place them in our hair. During the summer, the long branches and dark leaves provide cool shade for my patio.

Day 86

My mimosa tree reminds me that second chances are always possible. Our Father doesn't give up on us even when we give up on ourselves. Paul encourages, "I am certain that God, who began the good work within you, will continue his work until it is finally finished on the day when Christ Jesus returns," (Philippians 1:6). God continues to work in us when we falter, fail, and fall. Even when he painfully prunes away diseased areas of our life, his actions help us grow.

Perhaps you are struggling with the decision to start over. Maybe you tried a new endeavor and failed. Maybe you made a mess of your marriage. Maybe you got tired of trying to overcome a bad habit and simply gave up.

God wants you to know that it is never too late to start over. We only need to trust that he will provide the right growth in the right season as we continue to follow him. Like my mimosa, we can grow from the ground up and become something even more beautiful than before.

Father, thank you for continually working in my life. I am thankful that you never give up on me, even when I give up on myself. Help me learn from past mistakes so that I can move into new seasons of growth. Reveal areas of my life in which I have been afraid to move forward for fear of failure. Empower me to overcome hurtful patterns of speech, behavior, or thought. Give me the courage to start over as many times as needed until I walk in the fullness of your will for my life. In Jesus' name, Amen.

Personal Reflection

Prayerfully consider your attitude toward starting over or trying again when you fail. Think of a few noteworthy failures from your past and meditate on how you responded. What can you learn from your past that might help you move forward with greater success? Write your thoughts below.

Day 87
The Catalpa Tree

Yesterday I told you about my chocolate mimosa tree that grew back even after I had cut it down. Today I'd like to discuss my catalpa tree. Although not as beautiful as mimosas, catalpas are attractive shade trees with large leaves and small white flowers. To me, they look a bit quirky because of the long, thin seed pods that dangle among the leaves. Unfortunately, catalpas are invasive, which means they'll start sprouting everywhere if you aren't careful.

Thus, when a strong storm wind blew my catalpa over, I wasn't upset. We promptly cleaned up the mess, and I sprayed weed-killer on any remaining sprouts. My husband, Wesley, wanted to plant another tree in its place, but I was excited about the prospect of a sunny patch of garden. Since most of my garden is ensconced beneath shady trees, a full-sun area opened up new and exciting plant-related opportunities.

Just as the death of my first mimosa ushered in a new beginning, the demise of my catalpa tree opened up new possibilities. As with the mimosa, we sometimes need to start over to achieve an objective for which we originally hoped. As with the catalpa, however, the end of one thing often creates an opportunity to move in a completely different direction.

In Scripture, the prophet Joel described the fall of Judah and destruction of Jerusalem. The people faced unimaginable loss. They lost their homes, land, and their very way of life. Yet, even in the face of devastation and obliteration, God promised a new beginning. Joel proclaimed,

> *The Lord will reply,*
> *"Look! I am sending you grain and new wine and olive oil,*
> *enough to satisfy your needs.*
> *You will no longer be an object of mockery among the surrounding nations."*
>
> . . .
>
> *Don't be afraid, you animals of the field,*
> *for the wilderness pastures will soon be green.*
> *The trees will again be filled with fruit;*
> *fig trees and grapevines will be loaded down once more.*
> *Rejoice, you people of Jerusalem!*
> *Rejoice in the Lord your God!*
> *For the rain he sends demonstrates his faithfulness.*
> *Once more the autumn rains will come, as well as the rains of spring.*
> *The threshing floors will again be piled high with grain,*
> *and the presses will overflow with new wine and olive oil.*
>
> **Joel 2:19, 22–24**

So, what new direction might God be calling us to walk in today? Is he calling us to start over and try again where we failed in the past? Or is he calling us in an entirely different direction? Either way, as long as we overcome fear and move forward in faith, our Father will provide blessings that overflow and surpass our wildest dreams.

Day 87

Father, thank you for the promise of new opportunities. Teach me to walk in obedience so that I can experience every blessing you have prepared for my future. Empower me to overcome my fear and grow in faith. Give me wisdom to know when you are calling me to persevere in the same direction and when you are calling me to a new path. Help me to embrace each new journey with joy. In Jesus' name. Amen.

Personal Reflection

Re-read your personal reflection and notes from yesterday. Continue to meditate upon what you can learn from your response to past failures, endings, or losses. As God to reveal whether he might be calling you to try again in an area of failure or loss, or whether one area of your life might be ending so that you can seize a new opportunity.

_____

_____

_____

_____

_____

_____

_____

_____

_____

_____

Day 88
Praise & Worship

I can easily understand how people throughout history have fallen into the snare of worshiping nature. God's creation is stunningly beautiful and complex. Yet, to worship nature is to miss the greater truth to which it points. Paul teaches, "They know the truth about God because he has made it obvious to them. For ever since the world was created, people have seen the earth and sky. Through everything God made, they can clearly see his invisible qualities—his eternal power and divine nature. So they have no excuse for not knowing God," (Romans 1:19-20). Our Father loves us so much that he not only created a beautiful world for us to live in, but he reveals himself through creation. When we look at the world around us, we can see the power and love of our Father. And when we behold his glory, worship is the only appropriate response.

Indeed, that which we worship will become the touchstone around which we order our lives. Because God is the only entity that cannot be moved or shaken, worshiping him anchors our soul and creates a stable foundation for our lives. We don't worship God because *he* needs it, but because *we* need it. When we worship, we are reminded of his power, glory, and goodness. We are reminded that we are dependent upon him, and that he is fully capable of caring for us. We are reminded of his unconditional love and boundless grace.

Day 88

Each time we encounter his presence, our hearts are increasingly transformed and refreshed. The psalmist praises,

> Shout joyful praises to God, all the earth!
> Sing about the glory of his name!
> Tell the world how glorious he is.
> Say to God, "How awesome are your deeds!
> Your enemies cringe before your mighty power.
> Everything on earth will worship you;
> they will sing your praises,
> shouting your name in glorious songs."
> Come and see what our God has done,
> what awesome miracles he performs for people!
> He made a dry path through the Red Sea,
> and his people went across on foot.
> There we rejoiced in him.
> For by his great power he rules forever.
> He watches every movement of the nations;
> let no rebel rise in defiance.
> Let the whole world bless our God
> and loudly sing his praises.
> Our lives are in his hands,
> and he keeps our feet from stumbling.
> You have tested us, O God;
> you have purified us like silver.

Psalm 66:1–10

Let's join with the saints throughout history and all of creation in worshiping our Father today!

Father, thank you for protecting me and meeting all my needs. I praise you for your power, love, and grace. I worship you and confess my faith in you. I rejoice because your lovingkindness covers me and extends to every generation. I thank you for forgiving my sin and keeping my feet on solid ground. I ask you to test me and purify my heart. In Jesus' name, Amen.

Personal Reflection

Write your own psalm of praise to your Father. You don't have to be eloquent, but try to be specific. Thank God for the ways he has protected you and provided you. Praise him for his free gift of salvation and forgiveness. Express gratitude for the ways he has transformed your soul and your life. Finally, give him permission to test and purify your heart.

_____

_____

_____

_____

_____

_____

_____

_____

_____

_____

_____

Day 88

Day 89
Look at the Lilies

As we approach the end of our spring together, I want to revisit a subject we've discussed in several devotionals throughout this volume: worry. In fact, we began our journey together by discussing my carefree bluebirds, who remind us to rest in God's loving hands.

In Matthew 6, Jesus teaches about God's attentive care and exhorts us not to worry, which undermines our relationship with the Father. When we worry, we doubt God's love and his ability to provide. As a strategy for overcoming worry, our Savior recommends observing God's creation.

> *Look at the birds. They don't plant or harvest or store food in barns, for your heavenly Father feeds them. And aren't you far more valuable to him than they are? Can all your worries add a single moment to your life? And why worry about your clothing? Look at the lilies of the field and how they grow. They don't work or make their clothing, yet Solomon in all his glory was not dressed as beautifully as they are. And if God cares so wonderfully for wildflowers that are here today and thrown into the fire tomorrow, he will certainly care for you. Why do you have so little faith? So don't worry about these things, saying, "What will*

Day 89

> *we eat? What will we drink? What will we wear?" These things dominate the thoughts of unbelievers, but your heavenly Father already knows all your needs. Seek the Kingdom of God above all else, and live righteously, and he will give you everything you need.*
>
> **Matthew 6:26–33**

Our Savior tells us that when we seek to live according to the values God outlines in Scripture, our Father will meet every need. Jesus also implies that when we open our eyes to God's work in all creation, our faith will grow, and as our faith grows, our anxiety diminishes. So, let's make time to watch the birds, observe the lilies, and thank our Father for his generous provision in our lives.

Father, thank you for making yourself known through your creation. Teach me to slow down and open my eyes to your gracious provision throughout the natural world. As I seek to know you more, I ask you to grow my faith. Replace my worry with peace and my anxiety with confidence. In Jesus' name, Amen.

Personal Reflection

Your reflection today is two-fold. First, review your notes from days 2–4 and 43. Prayerfully meditate on whether you have made any progress. What strategies might you need to revisit to help you continue to grow in this area? Write your thoughts below. Second, find time in your schedule today or later in the week to take a "sensory stroll." Go for a walk outside and observe God's creation. Notice the sights, sounds, and smells with which your Father surrounds you. Meditate on God's gracious provision for the natural world and thank him for all the ways he cares for you.

Growth, Gardens, & Grace

Day 90
Faith Over Fear

As May 2022 approached, my heart was filled with dread. Asher would graduate from high school, and I would enter a new season of life as the parent of an adult. Based on my reaction to Asher starting kindergarten 13 years prior, I wasn't sure how I would handle the transition.

Despite my reluctance to have children, I doted upon my baby boys. From the outset, I absolutely loved being a mama. So, as Asher approached his *first* day of school, I became increasingly unsettled. I cried every time I thought about Asher leaving me, even if only for the duration of a school day. I didn't feel called to homeschool, which was much less common in those days, so I awaited his first day of school with a heavy heart.

As the day approached, I attended the pre-semester meet-and-greet with Asher's kindergarten teacher, and I completely fell apart. I sobbed uncontrollably until the kind-hearted lady finally stopped the meeting and helped me gather my wits. A few days later, as I prepared Asher's first-day lunchbox, I literally cried tears into his peanut butter and jelly sandwich.

Thus, as we approached the date of Asher's high school graduation, I feared a similar deterioration in my emotional and mental state. Thankfully, I navigated all graduation-related events with equanimity and fortitude.

I would like to say that my greater level of spiritual maturity carried me through the season, but in reality, I probably maintained my equilibrium because Asher didn't move away for college. He continued to live at home and work part-time as my ministry assistant. So, not much changed.

Yet, I'll confess that the thought of my boys growing up and moving away still fills my heart with fear. I don't know exactly what I'm afraid of because even when the boys move out, my schedule will still be full. It's not like I'm going to be sitting alone at home with nothing to do. Perhaps my fear arises from the unknown.

Throughout Scripture, our Father exhorts us not to fear. In Joshua 1:9, the Lord says, "Be strong and courageous! Do not be afraid or discouraged. For the Lord your God is with you wherever you go." The Father spoke these words of encouragement through Joshua to the nation of Israel as they approached the borders of the promised land . . . for the second time. The first time they'd approached the promised land, they had failed to enter. Their fear kept them from moving forward and taking hold of God's promises.

So, although I fear a future season of life, I will choose faith over fear. I won't let fear dictate my decisions or rule my thoughts. When fear encroaches upon my heart, I'll turn to the perfect love of my Father, which casts out all fear (1 John 4:18). I'll remind myself of his faithfulness in my past and his plans for my future (Jeremiah 29:11). I'll savor each day and abide in his presence. After all, tomorrow can worry about itself (Matthew 6:34)!

Father, thank you for blessing me in every season of my life. Teach me to savor my current season instead of worrying about my future. Forgive me for doubting your perfect will and unconditional love. Grow my faith and help me overcome my fears. When I am faced with the unknown, teach me to trust you with my future. Give me strength and courage as I seek to walk in your plans for my life. In Jesus' name, Amen.

Day 90

Personal Reflection

Prayerfully meditate on your future. Do you feel apprehensive or anxious about what the coming years might hold? Are you worried about any specific events or seasons of life? Confess any fears to your Father, then confess your faith over God's good plan for each season of your life. Read Isaiah 46:4, then write the verse on a notecard or type it into your phone. Memorize the verse so that you can remind yourself of God's love each time you are tempted to fear the future.

Scan the QR code for passages of Scripture

_____

_____

_____

_____

_____

_____

_____

_____

Growth, Gardens, & Grace

Day 90

www.ingramcontent.com/pod-product-compliance
Lightning Source LLC
Chambersburg PA
CBHW030142100526
44592CB00011B/1017